SEASONED
BY THE
SEA

We dedicate this book to our parents,
Jean and Vernon Amos,
who reside in Cape Breton, Nova Scotia,
and
Louise and (the late) Joseph Ahern.
All four of them have been unending sources of support and love for us.

Seasoned by the Sea

Delicious fish from the waters off
Cape Cod, Nantucket & Martha's Vineyard

Cynthia & Robert Ahern

The Peninsula Press

Cape Cod · Nantucket · Martha's Vineyard

Public domain marginalia from
Fishes, Volume 5 of The Nature Library
by David Starr Jordan & Barton Warren Evermann
Doubleday, Page and Company
(New York, NY: 1905)

Published by
The Peninsula Press · Cape Cod 02670 USA
Donald W. Davidson
Publisher

Visit The Peninsula Press online:
w w w . c a p e c o d r e a d e r . c o m

First published in 1994 by The Peninsula Press.

Library of Congress Control Number: 2002106536
Ahern, Cynthia & Robert.
    Seasoned by the Sea: Delicious Fish from the Waters off Cape Cod, Nantucket &
Martha's Vineyard
The Peninsula Press, ©2002.
Includes index and illustrations.
ISBN 1-883684-28-5
1. Cape Cod, Nantucket & Martha's Vineyard — Seafood.
2. Cape Cod, Nantucket & Martha's Vineyard — Cooking.
3. Cape Cod, Nantucket & Martha's Vineyard — Fisheries.

Third Edition
1 2 3 4 5 6 7 8 9 0 / 10 09 08 07 06 05 04 03 02

Foreword

I T GOES WITHOUT SAYING that Cape Cod, Nantucket & Martha's Vineyard all have changed greatly over the past three hundred years. Once a full day's journey from Boston, this peninsula and these islands now can be close enough in travel time to be a suburb of that city, complete with many of the same conveniences and inconveniences of the 21st Century.

But if you know where to look, you can still find slices of life that have more connections with the past than to the future. The world of the Cape & Islands fisherman is one of those places, and we are thankful every day that we are able to be connected to that world.

The fishermen with whom we deal are still rugged, self-sufficient individuals whose livelihood depends solely upon their ability to understand and survive the elements of nature. Their lives depend upon good judgment and quick-thinking on an unforgiving ocean. The food and shelter that they provide for their families only come if they are successful each day. They receive no unemployment benefits. They get no pay for sick days. They take no paid vacations. Instead, they must go to sea each day and prove their ability anew.

Meanwhile, they exist in every town on the Cape & Islands without a great deal of notice. Their boats range in size from skiffs of only sixteen feet to ships of a hundred feet or more. Their understanding of going to sea and returning with a saleable product has been carried on by generations of their forbearers: Nickersons, Bassetts, Bakers, Richardsons, and the like. They are not always easy to deal with, and they don't always agree with each other, but they *do* know how to fish.

We consider ourselves fortunate to be so connected to this old world amid a rapidly changing new one. We are forever thankful that we know about these people and that they continue to make these daily trips to the sea, then back to the shore so that we are able to sell the fruits of their labors.

This book is dedicated to all of these fishermen, from all of the towns on Cape Cod, Nantucket & Martha's Vineyard. But, in particular, it is dedicated to those from the port of Chatham.

Cecy & Bob Ahern
Chatham, Cape Cod
June, 2002

CECY AND BOB AHERN washed ashore on Cape Cod in 1972 and landed in Chatham, where they still live. Fresh out of college with degrees in English and Education, Bob found his part-time work in a fish market of greater use. For several seasons, he managed Swan River Fish Market, while Cecy worked at the Swan River Restaurant. They spent their winters travelling (collecting recipes all the while), commercially fishing, building their home, and raising two handsome sons.

Early on in the '80s, they had the good fortune to become owners of the Swan River Restaurant & Fish Market, which they continue to operate in its original coastal setting today. The original restaurant remains a seasonal business, but the fish market continues to operate throughout the year. A second Swan River Fish Market & Restaurant has been opened in Naples, Florida, and Swan River now supplies restaurants throughout Southern Florida with freshly-caught fish from the waters off Cape Cod, Nantucket & Martha's Vineyard.

Table of Contents

Appetizer
Gourmet Pizza with White Clam Sauce
Crab StuffedPortabello • Littlenecks Salerno

Soup
Shrimp Gumbo
Mackerel Soup in the Style of Provence • Crab Soup

Sandwich
Ginger Teriyaki Salmon Sandwich

Salad
Asian Noodle Salad with Grilled Shrimp

Entrées
Sole Oscar • Flounder Florentine with Cream Sauce
Mackerel en Papillote • Salmon in Filo with Scallion Remoulade
Mackerel with Sesame-Dijon Glaze
Smoked Salmon Primavera • Squid Bolognase

Shad Roe • Shrimp & Clams with Linguine
Linguine with White Clam Sauce • Scrod San Sebastian
Fillet of Sole with Shitake Champagne Sauce
Baked Whitefish with Herbs & Vegetables
Coho Salmon with Rice Stuffing

Appetizer
Mussels Diablo • Marinated Mussels
Three-Layer Seafood Terrine
Crabmeat Cocktail with Dijon Sauce
Crabmeat Spread on Toast Rounds • Smoked Fish Spread

Soup
Key West Conch Chowder

Salad
Seafood Pasta Salad • Calamari Salad
Swan River Shrimp Salad
Shrimp & Bowtie Pasta Salad • Grilled Fish Caesar Salad
Chilled Grilled Shrimp on Greens

Entrées
L.O.B. Grilled Fish
Chilled Poached Halibut with Dijon Sauce
Oriental Steamed Salmon • Blackened Salmon
Striped Bass in Filo with Red Pepper Mayonnaise
Grilled Swordfish • Seafood en Brochette
Grilled Yellowfin Tuna with Tomato Mint Sauce
Grilled Fresh Tuna with Rosemary Lime Marinade
Grilled Striped Bass with Fresh Fruit Salsa
Mako Shark Steak au Poivre • Bluefish Packets
Grilled Mahi-Mahi with Black Bean Salsa
Grilled Grouper en Brochette
Grilled Salmon Noisettes with Orange Mint Salsa

Appetizer

Smoked Bluefish Paté ♦ Broiled Oysters on the Half Shell
Oysters Rockefeller ♦ Steamed Oysters: West Coast Style
Stuffed Cherrystone Clams ♦ Cape Scallop Appetizer

Soup

Oyster & Spinach Stew ♦ Smoked Salmon Chowder
Cape Scallop Stew

Entrées

Mussels Steamed with Garlic & Wine ♦ Broiled Cape Scallops
Sole Almondine
Flounder Pinwheels with Mushroom Marsala Sauce
Baked Fish with Pesto ♦ Mussels Palermo
Lobster Pie ♦ Crabmeat Enchiladas ♦ Shrimp Burritos
Grilled Tuna with Wilted Greens & Balsamic Onions
Grouper with Sweet Potato Crust
Jerk Seasoned Halibut with Apple Ginger Chutney
Seafood Creole ♦ Paella ♦ Lobster Sauté

Appetizer

Portuguese Stuffed Mussels
Wrapped Shrimp with Basil & Prosciutto
Shrimp & Artichoke Hearts Wrapped with Bacon
Crabmeat Patrice ♦ Terry's Clams Casino
Smoked Salmon & Caviar Pizza
Shrimp Mousse in Filo Packets
Crab Stuffed Mushroom Caps

Soup

Spicy Seafood Stew • New England Fish Chowder
Dairy-Free Clam Chowder • Billi-bi

Entrées

Scrod Oreganata
Newburg Sauce • Seafood Newburg en Casserole
Mussels Marinara
Baked Swordfish with Rosemary Wine Butter
Sea Scallops Marsala • Sea Scallops Provençal
Creamed Finnan Haddie on Toast
Ocean Catfish Cacciatore
Baked Whole Haddock with Seafood Stuffing
Seafood Lasagna with Tomato Basil Béchamel
Cod Steaks with Sundried Tomato Butter
Cuban Mahi-Mahi Dinner
Baked Scrod with Mushroom Miso Sauce • Seafood Mornay

The Offshore Catch

THERE IS ONLY ONE PLACE to begin this cookbook about fish from the waters off Cape Cod, Nantucket & Martha's Vineyard, and that is with the Cape's historic namesake, the codfish.

Cod is scrod is schrod is cod. That takes care of the Number One question ever asked in any fish market.

Actually, scrod is (please take notes on this) a generic term for a small, white-fleshed, fillet of any number of different fish. By definition, it should be a fish that is small: 1 to 4 pounds when whole. Scrod can be cod, haddock, pollock, hake, or a number of other North Atlantic white-fish that flourish offshore in Georges Bank. In most fish markets throughout the Cape & Islands and New England, scrod is cod, unless it is otherwise noted, such as "scrod haddock". Right off the boat, in fact, cod is separated into three classifications: "scrod cod" (1 to 4 pounds each), "market cod" (4½ to 10 pounds each), and "large cod" (over 10 pounds).

From Boston to Boise, most cod found on the market today is caught by draggers or net. The boats used are out to sea for many days at a time. As a result, the fish is banged and bruised to the point that it is lucky to be dead. Often, a week goes by before the cod gets to the plate.

The cod which we receive at the Swan River Fish Market, however, is caught by the oldest method still in commercial use today: hook-fishing. Our cod fishermen use two traditional methods: tub trawling (with many hooks set on floats) and hand-jigging. For centuries, jigging was the only

Scrod is a generic term for a small, white-fleshed, fillet of cod, haddock, pollock, hake, or a number of other North Atlantic whitefish flourishing offshore in Georges Bank.

way to catch cod, and it still remains the best. It is very labor intensive, and it yields only about one percent of all the cod on the market today.

When hand-jigging, each fisherman uses a line with one, two, or three hooks on it. He can be anywhere from one mile to 75 miles out to sea in ocean depths of 100 to 600 feet. He simply drops his weighted hook and bounces it off the bottom until a codfish hits it. Then, in comes the fish, which is immediately cleaned, washed, and iced. Within a few hours, that fisherman has headed back for the Cape, Nantucket or the Vineyard. In our case, the fishermen land at Chatham or Harwichport, and the fish is brought to us for filleting the next day. *That* is fresh fish!

Unfortunately, cod is one of many in our local waters that are suffering from overfishing. During the past twenty years, fishing technology has advanced so much that the stocks of many species have been seriously depleted. Each year, I have seen the catches decline and the fishermen land fewer fish. This is certainly not due to the smallboat fishermen based on the Cape & Islands.

The huge fleets fishing out of Boston, New Bedford, and Gloucester have become far too efficient with their electronic fishfinders, bottom-scouring dragger nets, and other unimaginable changes in methods that have brought the North Atlantic fish stocks down to perilous levels. If all the fishermen taking cod and haddock were hook-fishing, we would never be in such a situation. Of course, if there were only bicycles, we wouldn't have any automobile accidents either. The real world intrudes.

Federal management plans have been underway for the past few years to limit the amounts of fish that can be taken from our waters. Restrictions have been placed on fishermen, large boat and small, which have created hardships for all; however, the cutbacks have been showing effects undreamed of five years ago. Georges Bank stocks of codfish, haddock, yellowtail flounder, and sea scallops, in particular, have been rebounding. Various plans are still being discussed to create a healthy, viable, sustainable fishery in the North Atlantic. More changes are predicted and feared. Individual Transferable Quotas (ITCs) – which give ownership of quota amounts to large boats and which lead to consolida-

For centuries, hand-jigging was the only way to catch cod, and it still remains the best. It is very labor intensive, and it yields only about one percent of all the cod on the market today.

tion of fishing rights in the hands of a few large corporations – are on the horizon. Smallboat fishermen throughout coastal New England are strongly opposed to this easy method of fish management, because it means more million-dollar, oversized, ten-days-at-sea fishing machines. Quotas on fish caught are but one way of ensuring there will be fish to harvest tomorrow. Hook-fishing in smallboats is another. If low-impact hook fishermen were encouraged as an alternative to those big boats, then high quality fresh fish would always be available to the customer.

We should appreciate the fact that cod is probably the most versatile of all our fish. It is absolutely delicious when prepared in the most simple of fashions: broiled quickly with a touch of butter, as well as salt and pepper on top. The best way to ruin cod is to cook it too long, and that is easy to do. A one-pound fillet of scrod, which will feed two average eaters, takes only 5 to 8 minutes under the broiler.

There are any number of wonderful tasting offshore finfish closely resembling cod. Most of these are still underutilized and unappreciated (except by gourmet chefs and fishermen's wives!) Cusk, pollock, ocean catfish, and hake, to name a few, are usually available for half the price of haddock and cod. Visitors to our market are always full of questions about these "unknown" species. With great interest, they always ask about them, but then they still purchase haddock or cod. What can I say?

Cusk and ocean catfish both come from the deep, unpolluted waters of Georges Bank, and they are somewhat firmer in texture than pollock and hake. All of these species are bycatches, caught incidentally, while the fishermen are targeting cod, haddock, or the so-called "flatfish", sole and flounder. These fish all are sold skinless and boneless in fillets that are generally 1 or 2 pounds each and 1½ inches thick.

Any of the recipes calling for haddock or scrod could be used with these species as well. Experiment. Buy according to availability. Pick out the freshest fish that day. You won't be disappointed. Not long ago, we ran a special in our restaurant on pan-blackened ocean catfish. Unheard of! Not to be found in any cookbook. (Yet!) But the taste and the response would have brought a smile to the face of any Cajun chef.

We should appreciate the fact that cod is probably the most versatile of all our local fish. It is absolutely delicious when prepared in the most simple of fashions.

Yet another great-tasting fish from our offshore waters is whiting, a small fish, weighing 1 to 1½ pounds when whole. Too small to fillet, whiting is generally cooked whole. Though it is served with the bone intact, the delicate, white meat flakes easily away from the bone, and the taste is absolutely worth the effort. In fact, you'll find that the flavor and the moisture make whiting one of the tastiest white fish.

One of the most unfortunate things about our American approach to eating fish is our paranoia about bones. In most of the world, fish is sold and cooked whole. I'll never forget the sight in the Mercado in Seville, Spain of fish stall after fish stall with all the fish displayed on ice, *whole!* The fish sold that day were steaked through from one side, but left attached at the bottom so that they could be splayed out like an accordion. As customers bought their steaks, the fishmongers would simply cut the rest of the way through, then bag them up.

The taste of fish cooked with bone and skin still intact really is so much better. Consider the contrast between a dry, baked chicken breast and a chicken roasted whole. Though so much of the flavor comes from the skin and the bone, we just can't seem to convince Americans. Only the Old World and ethnic cooks – whether Chinese, Japanese, Italian, Portuguese, or Greek – seem to appreciate this point!

Whiting was introduced to me by one of the Cape & Islands' most noted fishmongers, Cosmo Montagna. Cozzie operated a fish market for some thirty years out of the basement of a building he owned in Hyannis. One day I was driving a fish truck with freight for him, and after I delivered the whiting, he asked me if I had ever tasted the fish. "Of course not," I told him. I had been raised on fried haddock on Fridays (or fish sticks if times were bad.) "Well, don't worry about your next stop," he said. "Forget your waiting boss watching the clock. You're going to have a treat." Cozzie took three plump whiting, deftly cleaned out the entrails, floured them well, then fried them. What a taste! A revelation! Cozzie, I'll *always* be indebted to you!

> The taste of fish cooked with bone and skin intact really is so much better. Consider the contrast between a dry, baked chicken breast and a chicken roasted whole.

The Spring Catch

THE ADVENT OF SPRING should be reason enough for joy throughout the Cape & Islands, and it is. In the world of fresh fish, however, spring brings countless other reasons for us to smile. Our fish counter literally fills up with species we could only dream about in the winter. The ocean begins to warm, schools migrate north, clams rise up from their winter depths, fish spawn, the herring run. Changes, anticipated delights, cycles renewed. You've gotta love it!

One of the first signs of spring comes from the lowly herring's aristocratic relative, the shad. Shad roe, the egg sac of the bony shad fish, is a traditional spring meal in the Northeast. An acquired taste, to be sure, shad roe tops the list for many a Yankee.

Shortly after the shad arrive, our local trap fishermen set out their nets. This ancient form of fishing has died out in most regions. From our market, however, we can clearly see this fishery is still in active and productive use. The process involves driving 30-foot long poles into the sandy bottom from large open wooden boats. Nets are strung between the poles, which funnel migrating fish into a heart-shaped center. There the fish are trapped and live, until the boats bring them the few miles to shore. Nothing could be fresher. These weirs are only productive for two months each spring, but they yield hundreds of thousands of pounds of the highest quality fish.

The first fish caught in these weirs are squid, and the quality of this

One of the first signs of spring comes from the lowly herring's aristocratic relative, the shad.

15

catch is far superior to any caught by dragger boats. In draggers, squid get tossed and mangled, and they lose their best qualities before they get to the dock. Trap-caught squid are alive and at the dock within an hour or two. The boats unload a couple of miles from our market, so it is then only minutes before they are on ice for our customers!

Truly, one of the most amazing sights to be seen, better than tulips and daffodils popping up in spring, is the sight of a trap fisherman standing waist-deep amidst oozing squid in the middle of his trap boat. It is an unforgettable sight! Picture Captain Paul Lucas, a man of substantial girth, sailing up the Herring River to his dock. The boat's rails are only inches above the water. From stem to stern and across the entire deck, nothing but thousands of pounds of squid and *Captain Eelgrass*. When he needs to move from his wheel he just shifts into the squid and waits for the mass to fill in behind him. Words cannot describe!

The squid are still alive, and during their season the weather is always raw and damp on the waterfront. They are then hauled up onto the dock, loaded into barrels of iced saltwater, and trucked off to market. And *Captain Eelgrass* goes home to Squid Dreams.

Unfortunately, squid season only lasts three or four weeks. We try to freeze a few thousand pounds for use over the summer. In fact, the U. S. Department of Fisheries recommends freezing squid to tenderize it, and the fish loses nothing in quality (which is rare for seafood.)

Our next spring catch in the weir traps is mackerel. Again, the quality of trap mackerel far surpasses that of any other caught. These mackerel actually flush out their stomachs while trapped in these nets. There is no bait for them to eat. And the result is the highest quality fish of the year.

A fresh trap mackerel is lean, delicious, and not at all oily. When properly cooked, this fish will surprise fussy eaters with its mild taste. A wonderful and inexpensive source of both protein and flavor that has long been a valued food source in Europe and elsewhere, mackerel remains one of America's most underutilized fish resources.

Meanwhile, mackerel make an even shorter appearance in Nantucket

A fresh trap mackerel is lean, delicious, and not at all oily. When properly cooked, this fish will surprise fussy eaters with its mild taste.

and Vineyard Sounds than do squid. Driven out of these waters by that most voracious of predators, the bluefish, the mackerel migrate northward to Cape Cod Bay and the Gulf of Maine for the rest of the summer. Close on their tailfins in huge schools during late spring, the bluefish arrive, skinny and hungry from their long trip up from southern waters. They will be found in the sounds and bays throughout the summer, and often they linger until October if the weather stays warm.

Bluefish is another species which suffers from a bad reputation of its oily flavor. If the bluefish is fresh and properly handled, however, nothing could be further from the truth. Too often these fish are caught by sportfishermen, who bring ice for their beer, but not for their fish. Instead, their catch sits uncleaned and abused in the sun for hours. If cleaned and iced on the boat, however, then cooked within a day or two, fresh bluefish is delicious and full of flavor. If you've never done bluefish right, give it a try. You'll be pleasantly surprised.

Spring is also the season for flounder, a family of fish that represents dozens of varieties. Often called "flatfish", the members of the flounder family are different from other finfish simply because they are truly flat instead of round. While they are all hatched with a single eye on each side of the head, one eye travels over the top during maturity until it ends up right next to the other. The flatfish then inhabits the very bottom of the river or ocean, often burying itself in the mud and showing only those eyes. The most common flounder we sell include: yellowtail, blackback, dab, and fluke. Sole is another cousin of the flounder. The grey sole is one of our most popular fish; lemon sole is another we sometimes see.

Most of the flounder unloaded in our ports are caught by draggers, local boats that can fish anywhere from within sight of land to a hundred miles out on Georges Bank. While the days are over when draggers came into Boston and New Bedford with hundreds of thousands of pounds of flounder, perhaps our fisheries will see those days return. Meanwhile, many smallboat fishermen throughout the Cape & Islands are still able to bring in flounder each day to meet local needs. Even our longline fishermen hook some gorgeous blackbacks among the cod and pollock.

Often called "flatfish", the members of the flounder family are different from other finfish simply because they are truly flat instead of round.

Just yesterday, I saw 50 pounds of "slammers" being unloaded. Some weighed 4 to 5 pounds each. In fact, as I write this, tomorrow is the first of May, opening day of the recreational season for flounder fishing. Many blackback flounder have wintered in the Cape's rivers, such as Bass River and Parkers River in Yarmouth, Mitchell River in Chatham, as well as estuaries throughout Nantucket and Martha's Vineyard. All will be loaded with eager fishermen and hungry flounder.

Swan River itself is frequently a hot spot for flounder fishing. We have seen some beauties brought out right here at our little bridge on Lower County Road; however, it is more common to see eels caught here. That's when the entertainment gets good, as amateur anglers stare in horror at a fat, 18-inch eel squirming around on their line. If they try to grab the thing, the eel just wraps around their wrists, and . . . Oh well, I don't want to lose any cooks here.

The finest eating fish of all the flounder is the grey sole. It varies in size from 12 to 30 inches. From my experience, flounder (in general) and grey sole (in particular) are the most difficult of all fish to fillet; even a large fish is only 1 or 2 inches thick. From this, you have to cut two fillets and remove the skin. As a result, roughly two-thirds of the fish goes into the barrel. So, if you start with a whole fish costing $1 to $3 per pound, you don't need a calculator to see where the cost comes from with these fish. The sweet, fresh fillets make them well worth the price.

Spring is also a great time to get clams of all kinds. As the winter winds and ice give way to sunshine and longer daylight hours, the steamers and quahogs (pronounced *KOE-hogs*, please) rise up from their sandy depths. They are easier to dig, so suddenly all the hibernating shellfishermen appear with bushels of clean, meaty clams. And just as timely, folks start to think about their favorite shellfish.

Cape & Islands shellfishermen are a separate breed altogether. Self-proclaimed "River Rats", they are as independent and ornery as any cowboy who ever lived! I love them. They usually have very little in the way of material goods to show for their toil. They have little use for traditions of modern day. They love their independence, they could never

Cape & Islands shellfishermen are a separate breed altogether, as independent and ornery as any cowboy who ever lived!

deal with bosses or time-clocks, and they can hardly stand each other (related or not) as they team up in short-term alliances. But few people in any field of work put in as hard a day as do our local shellfishermen. And let me warn you: if a local shellfisherman challenges you to arm wrestle, graciously defer! All that mud-digging is a better workout than any body-building regimen I know.

Cape Cod, Nantucket & Martha's Vineyard benefit from being some of the most shellfish rich areas along the entire Atlantic seaboard. With the exception of Chesapeake Bay, we are one of the furthest points south for finding steamers (softshell clams), and we are the furthest point north for native quahogs (hardshell clams). We also have in abundance sea (surf) clams, to which we can add our fabulous oysters, scallops, blue mussels, razor clams, and conchs to complete a shellfish lover's heaven.

One of the first methods of employment I sought out on Cape Cod was that of a shellfisherman. (I would have to get humorist Dave Barry to write that book, funnier than fiction.) But I learned a lot. I firmly believe that you have to be born to that sort of work. Oh, I did make some money at it. No denying that. In fact, we often say that we built the house we live in with Cape scallops! Back in the 70s there was some great money to be made harvesting scallops; even for a greenhorn, washashore. I loved it, and it was hard for me to believe that it was a job.

We would set out at sunrise in a 20-foot boat, always in the fall, and we would drag along river and bay bottom in one of the prettiest places upon this earth. We would haul-up our small dredges by hand, then cull out the money catch (bay scallops) from dinner (flounders, monkfish, clams, and whatever). And we always kept a 5-gallon bucket full of sea-water, into which went all the specimens for our 55-gallon aquarium back home. Sure, it was work. Our aching backs attested to that each night. But how could you measure the benefits of coming home with all those treats, a sunburned and salty smile, *plus* a pocket full of cash? Maybe someday I'll retire healthy and return to a little shellfishing as a pastime.

So much for Scallop Dreams. Clams are a little different. Quahogs are at their greatest abundance in the spring. The winter causes them to

The Cape & Islands benefit from being one of the most shellfish rich areas along the entire Atlantic seaboard.

burrow deeply, and the clam flats are often inaccessible because of ice and rough waters. I know firsthand that trying to make a living digging clams in winter is difficult. More than one lean January I waded waist deep into 35° water with a stiff wind piercing unseen openings in my gear and tried to put bread on the table with clam profits. If clams were priced as precious metals I would have been all set. I will have to say that it was character-building and leave it at that.

In spring, clams rise to the surface of their muddy homes. Spring-time, and the diggin' is easy! Who wouldn't mind going out in that clear, warming air, soaking up the sights and sounds along the shore, playing in the mud, then going home with a decent day's pay?

A quahog is sold in three different sizes. The smallest legal size qua-hog is a "littleneck clam". Measuring a minimum of 1 inch in thickness, littlenecks are either eaten raw on the half shell, or used whole in the shell for various soups and stews. The next grading for a quahog is a middle size called a "cherrystone", measuring 2½ to 3 inches in diameter. Cherrystones are also popular eaten raw. As a quahog gets older and larger, however, it becomes a "chowder clam". Measuring above 3½ inches, these clams are too big to be enjoyed raw, so they are generally shucked and used in various recipes calling for chopped clams. The quahog has a much more intense flavor than the other clams mentioned, but a truly good clam chowder must have some quahog in it.

The sea clam is a large softshell clam found in deeper waters. It has a much different flavor, sweeter and milder than a quahog, and they are often cut for so-called clam "strips" without the bellies (as opposed to "whole" fried clams). Though they are delicious, a chowder made only from sea clams would be like making spaghetti out of a can of *Franco-American*.

Sea clams are generally brought in by 60-foot boats working close to shore. A day's catch might be 200 bushels. Then comes the delightful job of shucking them. We used to shuck them in our market. Now, however, the Commonwealth requires elaborate shucking premises, and we lack the space. So we get ours shucked in Chatham.

The quahog has a more intense flavor than other clams, but a truly good clam chowder must have some quahog in it.

The number of products made from sea clams is impressive. They are used in chowders, clam pies, frying strips, "clam tenders," and clam fritters, just to name a few. And even the shells are put to good use. Throughout the Cape & Islands, they are not only found inside cottages as ashtrays, but also outside to line walkways and driveways with their quaint white appearance. Aside from looking nice, they also let rainwater leach through, thus providing a far more ecologically sound surface than pavement. A classic example of early Yankee recycling!

One of the tastiest spring arrivals is the crab, which could almost be considered an underutilized species from local waters. We have two types of edible crabs: blue crabs and rock crabs. Blue crabs are not fished commercially in our waters, and the only commercial operation I know of is in another part of southeastern Massachusetts. While blues are the pride of the Chesapeake, they are still quite plentiful in our rivers and bays. In fact, crabbing remains a popular pastime, and often families make a day of trying to catch the pesky critters.

Rock crabs, on the other hand, are caught commercially, and bear close resemblance in both taste and appearance to the legendary stone crabs of Florida. Rock crabs are intertidal, meaning they are found in deeper saltwater, as opposed to the blue crabs found in the shallower, brackish waters of the estuaries. Rock crabs are considered a bycatch of lobstering, and often the lobstermen just throw them back. For one thing, rock crabs are difficult to handle without having the crab handle you. And then once they have been landed and cooked, the battle is only half over. After all, they are not called "rock" crabs, because they play guitars! Shucking them requires a mallet or heavy knife, plus a lot of patience. All that said, however, the result is well worth it. Many people prefer the sweet meat from these crabs over lobster meat.

I think that one of the saddest developments in the world of food technology must certainly be that mock crabmeat sold in supermarkets as "seafood salad", also known as surimi. It's a crabmeat product, which contains mostly fish, along with lots of sugar, red food dye, and 15 per cent crabmeat and crab shells. This ubiquitous product is being served all

One of the tastiest spring arrivals is the crab, which could almost be considered an underutilized species from local waters.

over the country in the guise of crabmeat, crab stuffing, and other so-called "crab" recipes.

That's really a shame, not only because quality is being sacrificed for profit, but also because the public's taste for the real thing is being altered. So, when people say that food doesn't taste as good as it did in the old days, I couldn't agree more. So much of our food today is altered. Seafood appeals to us in part, because most of it is still a natural product, the same today as it was centuries ago . . . if you are buying it prudently.

Spring on the Cape & Islands clearly brings an abundance of seafood to the tables. My old friend, mentor, fishing partner, and fellow fishmonger, the late George Vining of George's Fish Market in Harwichport often would say: "There's no reason for any able-bodied person to either go hungry or go wanting for work on Cape Cod. The shores around us are full of opportunity."

Opportunity not to get rich necessarily, but certainly to eat as a King!

Seafood appeals to us in part, because most of it is still a natural product, the same today as it was centuries ago . . . if you are buying it prudently.

A Spring Menu

Appetizer
Gourmet Pizza with White Clam Sauce
Crab Stuffed Portabello
Littlenecks Salerno

Soup
Shrimp Gumbo
Mackerel Soup in the Style of Provence
Crab Soup

Sandwich
Ginger Teriyaki Salmon Sandwich

Salad
Asian Noodle Salad with Grilled Shrimp

Entrées
Sole Oscar
Flounder Florentine with Cream Sauce
Mackerel en Papillote
Mackerel with Sesame-Dijon Glaze
Salmon in Filo with Scallion Remoulade
Smoked Salmon Primavera
Squid Bolognase

Shrimp & Clams with Linguine
Shad Roe
Linguine with White Clam Sauce
Scrod San Sebastian
Fillet of Sole with Shitake Champagne Sauce
Baked Whitefish with Herbs & Vegetables
Coho Salmon with Rice Stuffing

Gourmet Pizza
with White Clam Sauce

B OB AND I THANK OUR CHEF, Glen Woodworth, for this clever variation on the pizza theme, which can be served as an hors d'oeuvre for a crowd, or a filling lunch for four to six people.

Pizza dough is not really difficult to make. Before you roll out the pizza dough, consider how you will use the recipe. You may wish to make one big, rectangular crust, or else round individual pizzas.

This sauce can be made using all quahogs or a combination of half quahogs/half sea clams, which is what we prefer. The quahogs have a full, salty flavor, while the sea clams are somewhat sweeter and more bland. Whatever you decide, if the clams are not available in half-pints, you could make a double batch and freeze whatever you don't use.

FOR THE PIZZA DOUGH:

1 cup lukewarm water *¼ teaspoon black pepper*
1 teaspoon sugar *¼ teaspoon salt*
1 packet of yeast *½ teaspoon each: onion powder,*
2 tablespoons olive oil *garlic powder, crushed red pepper*
3½ cups flour *& oregano*

FOR THE CLAM SAUCE:

4 tablespoons olive oil *1 pint clam juice*
3 cloves of garlic, chopped *1 teaspoon oregano*
1 cup chopped onion *1 teaspoon basil*
½ pint chopped quahogs *1 tablespoon fresh parsley*
½ pint chopped sea clams *Fresh ground black pepper*

25

FOR THE TOPPING:

Grated mozzarella cheese   *Dried oregano*
Sliced fresh tomatoes

TO MAKE THE PIZZA DOUGH:

Stir the sugar into the warm water, then add the yeast and mix until it is dissolved. Let it sit for 5 minutes to activate.

Combine the dry ingredients in a large mixing bowl. Add the oil to the yeast mixture, then pour it into the flour mix, stirring until all the flour is incorporated. Turn the dough onto a lightly-floured surface and knead it for 5 minutes. Return the dough to the mixing bowl, cover it with a clean, damp cloth, and set it in a warm, draft-free place to rise for one hour or until it is about double its original size.

Using a rubber spatula, turn the dough out onto a lightly-floured surface. Knead it briefly, then divide it into four equal segments, forming each into a ball. Cover them with a damp towel and allow them to rest for 10 minutes before rolling them out.

Preheat the oven to 400° F.

Using a lightly-floured rolling pin, roll out each dough ball to a ¼-inch thickness then place on a sheet pan to bake. Bake for 10 to 15 minutes or until the top is golden brown in places and puffed-up well.

TO MAKE THE SAUCE:

In a large skillet, heat the oil. Add the garlic and onion, then cook on medium heat until the onions are clear. Add the clams and cook for 5 minutes, stirring occasionally. Pour in the clam juice and herbs, then bring to a gentle boil. If you won't be using the sauce right away, turn off the heat to prevent overcooking the clams and making them tough.

TO ASSEMBLE THE PIZZAS:

Ladle clam sauce onto the cooked pizza shell. Cover with a light layer of cheese, then top each pizza with several tomato slices and a sprinkling of oregano. Bake on a sheet pan for 10 to 15 minutes until the cheese begins to brown and bubble.

Remove the pizza to a cutting board, cut into slices and serve.

Your oven can be the perfect place to raise dough. Turn the oven to 200°F for a minute, then turn it off. Open the door for a few minutes to cool it down, then place the dough inside and close the door. Just remember not to turn on the heat while the dough is in it!

Crab Stuffed Portabello

STUFFED PORTABELLO MUSHROOMS can be used as a first course or served on a thick slice of toast as an open faced sandwich.

6 large portabellos	1 shallot, diced
½ pound crabmeat	¼ cup sherry
2 tablespoons butter	½ cup mayonnaise
2 teaspoons minced garlic	¼ cup Parmesan cheese
¼ cup diced celery	¼ teaspoon fresh ground black pepper
4 cups stale French bread, chopped or torn into ½-inch chunks	

Preheat oven to 400° F. Remove stems from mushrooms and cut them into ¼-inch cubes. Wipe the caps with a damp paper towel, brush them with a little melted butter and place them, stem side down on a sheet pan. Cook in the oven for 5 minutes, then set them aside to cool.

Melt the butter in a sauté pan. Add in the chopped stems, shallots, celery and garlic. Cook on medium heat for a few minutes until shallots are clear. Add in the sherry and remove from the heat.

Put the bread pieces in a mixing bowl and pour the vegetable mix over them. Mix to distribute the liquids and allow it to cool.

Check the crabmeat for shell bits, then add it, the mayonnaise, Parmesan and pepper to the stuffing. Divide the stuffing mix among the mushroom caps, packing it slightly so that it will hold together. Sprinkle the top with Parmesan cheese and paprika.

Bake at 400° F for 15 minutes or until heated through.

Littlenecks Salerno

Serves 4

WHEN THE WEATHER warms up in spring, clam diggers can't resist the call of the mud flats. Here's a nice reward for the hunter and gatherer in your family.

> *32 littlenecks, rinsed*
> *2 cups beer*
> *1 cup water*
> *1 pound chourico*
> *2 tablespoons fresh chopped basil*

Put all the ingredients into a saucepan. Cover and cook on high heat for about 10 minutes or until all the shells are open.

Serve with plenty of crusty French bread.

Shrimp Gumbo

Serves 6

THERE'S PLENTY OF FIREPOWER in this soup! Adjust the cayenne pepper for a milder blend. A bottle of Tabasco on the table should placate those who think you may have overreacted to the cautionary note.

1½ pound medium shrimp, peeled and deveined*

1½ cups uncooked rice	*3 cups seafood stock, hot*
3 tablespoons olive oil	*¼ teaspoon white pepper*
2 tablespoon flour	*1 tablespoon gumbo filé powder*
½ cup diced onion	*¼ teaspoon cayenne*
½ cup diced green pepper	*½ teaspoon black pepper*
½ cup diced celery	*½ teaspoon garlic powder*
8 ounces andouille sausage	*½ teaspoon thyme*
1 15-ounce can crushed tomatoes	*Salt to taste*
	Fresh chopped parsley for garnish

Measure the white pepper, filé powder, cayenne, black pepper, garlic powder and thyme into a small dish and set aside.

Cook the rice in 3 cups of water to which ½ teaspoon of salt has been added. Keep it hot to serve with the gumbo.

In a large saucepan or Dutch oven heat the oil, then cook the onion, pepper, and celery until they are quite browned. Add in the spices and mix briefly before adding in the flour.

Stir the hot stock into the pot, then add the tomatoes and sausage.

*See Kitchen Notes

Allow the mixture to simmer for 30 minutes, then add in the shrimp.

Cook for an additional 10 minutes, then ladle the gumbo into shallow soup plates.

Form the rice into mounds by compressing it into a custard cup or shallow coffee mug. Place the rice in the center of each serving, sprinkle with fresh chopped parsley and serve.

Mackerel Soup
in the Style of Provence

Serves 6

PICTURE YOURSELF in a little cafe by the sea in France where all styles of fish soup begin with a rich stock and end with crusty garlic aïoli croutons. Various combinations are given different names, but all are bathed in the same piping hot broth. Our adaptation uses mackerel, chosen for its robust flavor. *Bon Appétit!*

1 loaf French bread	*1 cup roasted garlic aïoli*
6 mackerel fillets	*Fresh basil for garnish*

FOR THE ROASTED GARLIC AÏOLI:

1 head garlic	*Pinch of white pepper*
1 egg yolk	*1 tablespoon lemon juice*
Pinch of salt	*¾ cup olive oil*

FOR THE SOUP:

1 bulb fennel, chopped	*1 teaspoon thyme*
1 onion, chopped	*4 threads saffron*
3 cloves garlic, minced	*½ teaspoon white pepper*
3 tablespoon olive oil	*1 tablespoon fresh parsley, chopped*
3 cups fish stock	*1 bay leaf*
½ cup white wine	*2 tablespoons tomato paste*
3 cups water	*3 medium potatoes, peeled & chopped*

TO PREPARE THE ROASTED GARLIC AÏOLI:

Remove the loose outer skin from the head of garlic. Slice across the top so the tips of the cloves are exposed. Place the garlic in a very small oven-proof dish and add water until it is about half way up the head. Cover and bake for half an hour. Remove cover and continue roasting for another half hour. Allow the garlic to cool before proceeding with the next steps.

Squeeze the garlic cloves out of their skins and purée them in a blender.

Add the egg yolk, salt, pepper, and lemon juice, then process until smooth. With the machine still running, add the oil in a slow steady stream until the mixture reaches the consistency of mayonnaise.

Scrape down the sides of the bowl and process again briefly.

Refrigerate until needed.

TO PREPARE THE SOUP:

In a large pot, heat the oil and cook the garlic, onions and fennel until the onions are clear. Add in all the remaining ingredients and simmer gently until the potatoes are quite soft, about 30 minutes.

Remove the bay leaf and process in the blender until completely puréed. Add salt to taste.

TO PREPARE THE FISH:

Preheat oven to 400° F Lay the fillets skin side down on a baking sheet or broiler pan. Brush lightly with olive oil and sprinkle with salt, pepper, and lemon juice. Cook for 10 to 15 minutes until fish is *just* cooked through. Allow the fish to cool before removing bones and separating meat from the skin. Flake the cooked fish and set aside until needed.

TO PREPARE THE CROUTONS:

Cut the loaf diagonally to make 12 slices about ¾-inch thick. Brush both sides with olive oil and toast in the oven until they are quite crisp.

TO SERVE THE SOUP:

Distribute the flaked fish into 6 shallow soup bowls. Ladle hot broth over each Put a generous dollop of garlic aíoli on each crouton and prop them onto the rim of the dish, partly submerged in the soup. Garnish with finely sliced fresh basil.

Crab Soup

Serves 4 to 6

CELEBRATE SPRING and the return of fresh crabmeat with this aromatic blend of flavors.

1 pound fresh crabmeat	½ cup cooked corn
2 cloves garlic, minced	4 cups hot fish stock*
½ cup diced onion	1 tablespoon tomato paste
½ cup diced carrot	1 bay leaf
½ cup diced celery	1 teaspoon dried thyme
2 tablespoons olive oil	1 tablespoon Worcestershire sauce
2 teaspoon flour	¼ teaspoon white pepper
1 cup diced potatoes,	¼ cup sherry
steamed until tender	1 tablespoon fresh chopped Italian parsley
	2 teaspoons horseradish

Heat a large saucepan, add in the olive oil, then the garlic, onion, pepper, carrot and celery. Cook on medium heat, stirring frequently until the vegetables are lightly browned.

Sprinkle in the flour and stir to mix. Add in the broth slowly, stirring well to prevent the flour from forming lumps. Add the bay leaf, thyme, Worcestershire sauce, pepper, and tomato paste.

Simmer gently for 10 minutes, then add the potatoes, corn, crabmeat, sherry, and horseradish, but treat the soup gently so you don't pulverize the crab chunks. Continue cooking, about 10 minutes until the soup is steaming hot. Toss in chopped parsley at the last minute and serve.

*See Kitchen Notes

Ginger Teriyaki Salmon
Sandwich

BAKED OR GRILLED, this salmon sandwich is a great change of pace. You'll need bread with some substance; pass over the wimpy sliced white bread and select a hearty roll. You won't regret it!

FOR EACH PERSON, ALLOW:
> *5 ounce piece fillet of salmon*
> *Ginger teriyaki sauce**
> *Bermuda onion, sliced thin*
> *Romaine lettuce, sliced*
> *Mayonnaise (optional)*
> *Crispy French bread or Kaiser roll.*
>
> ** Look for bottled sauce at your fish market or in the Asian food section of most grocery stores.*

Marinate the salmon briefly in the teriyaki sauce. Preheat oven to 400° F. Bake the fish for 20 minutes, then test to be sure it is cooked through.

Spread mayonnaise on toasted rolls, then stack lettuce, onion, and a piece of fish on each.

Grab a handful of napkins and enjoy!

Asian Noodle Salad
with Grilled Shrimp

Serves 4 to 6

DELICIOUS with shrimp, scallops *or* crabmeat, this salad can be a lunch entrée, a side salad, or an offering on the buffet table.

> *3 or 4 shrimp or scallops per person*
> *1 package fresh Asian noodles*
> *Mixed greens*
> *1½ cups mixed slivered vegetables (radishes, scallions, carrots, pea pods, red, yellow or green peppers)*
> *1 tablespoon fresh chopped ginger*
> *2 cloves garlic, minced*
> *¼ cup peanut oil*
> *4 drops sesame oil*
> *2 tablespoons soy sauce*
> *1 tablespoon chopped fresh cilantro*
> *2 tablespoons sesame seeds, white, black or mixed*

FOR THE MISO VINAIGRETTE:
> *2 tablespoons miso*
> *¼ cup tarragon vinegar*

Brush the shrimp or scallops with vegetable oil, sprinkle with salt and pepper, then cook on the grill, 2 or 3 minutes per side.

Cook the noodles according to package directions, drain and rinse with cold water. Keep the noodles in ice water until you are ready to assemble the salad.

For ease during the grilling, you might want to put the seafood and vegetables on a few skewers.

35

Cut the vegetables, and add them to the (drained) noodles, with the oils, cilantro, and soy sauce. Arrange on a bed of greens. Drizzle the miso dressing over the greens, top the noodles with the seafood, then sprinkle with sesame seeds.

Buffet table option: Instead of big showy shrimp on top, use smaller shrimp and mix them right in.

Sole Oscar

Serves 4

TIMING IS IMPORTANT, so I recommend that you assemble all of the ingredients and necessary appliances, then plan to make the Hollandaise while the fish and asparagus are cooking. Though the sauce should be kept warm, it does contain uncooked eggs and must not be held for long.

For those who may wish to do without Hollandaise, this can still be a wonderfully satisfying, as well as a low cholesterol meal, if served with a juicy lemon wedge on the side.

> *4 medium to large sole fillets*
> *4 ounces of crabmeat*
> *12 stalks of asparagus*

FOR A FOOL-PROOF HOLLANDAISE SAUCE:

> *2 egg yolks*   *Pinch of white pepper*
> *Dash of salt*   *2 tablespoons lemon juice*
> *¾ cup of drawn butter**

TO PREPARE THE FISH AND ASPARAGUS:

Preheat the oven to 400° F.

Arrange a single layer of sole in a shallow baking dish. Spread the crabmeat over the fillets, add a few tablespoons of water to the pan, then cover it with foil wrap. If you have used a metal pan, the fish will cook in about 10 minutes. A glass or ceramic dish takes longer to heat up, so

*See Kitchen Notes

your dinner may take 20 minutes. In either case, sole is a delicate item and should not be overcooked. Take a peek under the foil to check for doneness. The fish will flake easily and be opaque throughout when it is finished.

As the fish bakes, steam the asparagus in a frying pan until it's tender.

To prepare a fool-proof hollandaise sauce:

Put the egg, lemon juice, salt and pepper into a blender and process briefly. While the blade is running, slowly drizzle in the butter. Continue to blend for a moment longer and *Voilà!* You've made a great Hollandaise.

To present each serving:

Carefully lift the fish onto individual plates. Lay 3 pieces of asparagus on top of each, then ladle a generous serving of sauce across it.

Flounder Florentine
with Cream Sauce

Serves 4 to 6

2 pounds of fillets provide six small or four medium portions

FOR THE SPINACH MIX:

One 10-ounce package of frozen, chopped spinach or one package of fresh spinach	½ cup bread crumbs
	¼ cup Parmesan cheese
	Pinch of nutmeg
2 tablespoons butter or margarine	Splash of Pernod
¼ cup onion, diced fine	Salt and pepper to taste

FOR THE CREAM SAUCE:

4 tablespoons butter or margarine	1 cup milk or cream
4 tablespoons flour	Dash of Tabasco sauce
1 cup fish stock*	Dash of Worcestershire sauce
	Salt to taste

TO MAKE THE SPINACH STUFFING:

Melt the butter in a small sauté pan and add the onions. Cook on medium heat until the onions are clear.

Clean the spinach. Frozen spinach must be defrosted and squeezed dry; fresh spinach must have stems and tough leaves removed, then be steamed before chopping. Place all the remaining ingredients in a bowl and mix together with the cooked onions and butter.

TO MAKE THE SAUCE:

In a small saucepan, melt the butter. Add the flour and cook together

*See Kitchen Notes

on medium heat, stirring constantly for about 5 minutes. Add the Tabasco and Worcestershire to the fish stock, then pour it slowly into the flour mix, stirring all the while with a wire whisk to eliminate lumps. Add the cream in the same manner, then reduce the heat and let the sauce cook for 5 to 10 minutes, stirring frequently until it thickens.

Preheat the oven to 400° F.

There are a variety of ways to prepare the dish from this point. You may wish to place some stuffing on the fillet and roll it for baking, or you may prefer to lay a fillet in the pan, spread some spinach mix upon it, then top it with another piece of fish. I have also used this stuffing with larger fillets, such as scrod, haddock, or whiting. In that case, I create a pocket by making a diagonal cut down from the top of the fillet, then stuff the pocket with the spinach mix.

In any case, place your fish in a shallow baking pan, cover it with foil and bake it for 10 minutes.

Remove the fish from the oven, ladle the warm sauce over it, sprinkle with a little Parmesan cheese, then return it uncovered to the oven for 5 to 10 minutes. The time in the oven depends upon the thickness of the fish and the temperature of your own oven, so be certain to check for doneness.*

*See Kitchen Notes

Mackerel en Papillote

FOR EACH PERSON, ALLOW:
> *1 large or 2 small mackerel fillets*
> *Thinly-sliced onion*
> *1 tablespoon of sherry*
> *Salt and pepper*
> *Parchment paper or aluminum foil*

Preheat the oven to 400° F.

For each serving, fold a piece of parchment paper in half and cut an elongated semi-circle 2 or 3 inches larger than the individual fillets. Open out the folded paper and place a serving of fish upon it, near the fold. Top with a thin onion slice, sprinkle the onion with a tablespoon of sherry, then season with salt and pepper. Fold down the other half of the parchment and crimp together the top and bottom edges to make a packet.

Place the packets on a baking sheet and cook for 10 to 15 minutes, depending upon the size of the fillets.

Packets may be placed on individual plates and opened with a knife at the table. The aroma of the escaping steam is part of the enjoyment of a fish cooked in parchment. (You may wish to tell your guests that they don't need to eat the paper.)

Salmon in Filo
with Scallion Remoulade

THIS IS ELEGANT FARE for entertaining or jazzing up a family dinner. Filo dough is readily available in the freezer of most grocery stores. For best results, allow it to defrost for 24 hours in your refrigerator. While it does have a reputation for being temperamental, filo can be managed quite well with a little practice and patience. I am always grateful that there are so many sheets in one box; if one or two of them tear or dry out, there are still plenty left. The results are always spectacular and worth the effort!

Fish in filo can be prepared up to a day before it is baked. Place the wrapped pieces on a baking sheet in the refrigerator. Cover loosely. Cook according to directions when needed.

FOR EACH PERSON, ALLOW:

6 to 8 ounces of skinless salmon fillet

Scallion greens, cut into ¼-inch lengths
Melted butter or margarine

FOR 1¼ CUPS OF SCALLION REMOULADE:

2 egg yolks	*Pinch white pepper*
2 tablespoons lemon juice	*1 tablespoon parsley, chopped*
1 teaspoon lemon rind, grated	*¼ cup chopped scallions*
Dash of salt	*1 cup salad oil*

Put all the ingredients for the remoulade, except for the oil, into a blender and process briefly to mince the herbs. In a slow, steady stream, pour the oil into the blender while it is running. When all the oil has been added, stop the blades to scrape down the sides of the container. Process for another thirty seconds to be sure the sauce is thoroughly blended, then refrigerate.

To prepare the filo packets:

Carefully unfold the filo dough onto a clean work space. Keep a clean, dampened kitchen towel handy to lay over the unused sheets in case you are interrupted, or they begin to dry while you are working.

Peel off a sheet of the dough, lay it on the counter and brush it with melted butter. Lay another sheet of dough on top of the first, brush it with melted better, and repeat the procedure. Cut the three layers in half widthwise.

Place a piece of fish on the filo dough about 2 inches in from the long side of the rectangle. Sprinkle a few scallions on the fillet, then begin to wrap by lifting the 2-inch edge of filo up to the fish and rolling the dough and fish over once. Pick up the flaps of dough on either side and fold them onto what is now the top. Continue to roll the fish and filo, keeping the edges tucked in, until you have run out of dough.

Place the packet onto a buttered sheet pan and make sure that the edge of dough is tucked under the fish. Ideally, the scallions will have ended up on top of the fish. If not, adjust the original placement of the next fillet onto the filo. Lightly brush the top of each packet with butter.

Bake in a preheated 375° F oven for 20 to 25 minutes until the dough is well-browned.

Serve with a generous dollop of scallion remoulade on the side.

Mackerel
with Sesame-Dijon Glaze

A SNAP TO PREPARE, this recipe gives mackerel a tasty lift!

FOR EACH PERSON, ALLOW:
8 to 10 ounces of mackerel

Blending together equal parts of mayonnaise and Dijon mustard, mix as much glaze as you will need. Place the fish in a shallow baking dish for broiling. Spread the glaze on the fish, then sprinkle with sesame seeds.

Place under the broiler (not too close to the heat) and cook for 5 to 10 minutes.

Check often to see that the top is not cooking too quickly. If it is, move it further from the heat and continue cooking until the flesh flakes easily with a fork.

Smoked Salmon Primavera

Serves 4

1 package fresh fettucine (or 8 ounces dry)

CHOOSE 4 OR 5 OF THE FOLLOWING VEGETABLES:
  *2 cups total: thinly-julienned broccoli, carrots, zucchini,
   summer squash, red or green peppers, or mushrooms*

4 tablespoons olive oil   *1 tablespoon parsley, chopped*
3 cloves of garlic, minced   *2 scallions, cut into ¼-inch pieces*
1 small onion, in thin wedges   *12 black olives, sliced in thirds*
2 cups light cream   *½ cup Parmesan cheese*
Fresh ground black pepper   *8 ounces smoked salmon*
1 teaspoon basil

Prepare the fettucine according to package directions, but undercook it slightly. Set it aside.

In a 10-inch skillet, heat 2 tablespoons of the oil. Add the garlic and onions, then sauté on medium heat until the onions are clear. Add in the rest of the oil, as well as your selection of julienned vegetables, tossing the pan a few times so they will be coated with the oil. Pour in a quarter cup of water, cover and cook on medium heat for 5 minutes. To retain their color and just a little crispness, the vegetables should be lightly cooked.

Add in the cooked fettucine, cream, cheese, pepper, and basil.

When this mixture is heated through, add in all of the remaining ingredients, except for a few olive slices and some parsley for garnish.

Gently stir the mixture to prevent breaking up the fish pieces and continue cooking on medium to low heat until it is hot throughout.

Turn the primavera onto a warmed platter or individual plates, garnish with olives and parsley, then serve.

Squid Bolognase

WITH GARLIC TOAST ROUNDS, this may be used as an appetizer for 6; over pasta, this recipe can serve as an entrée for 4.

FOR EITHER USE:

1 pound squid*	½ teaspoon oregano
1 clove of garlic, minced	½ teaspoon thyme
1 medium onion, diced	½ teaspoon basil
2 tablespoons olive oil	½ tablespoon parsley, chopped
1 28-ounce can plum tomatoes, well-drained and chopped	½ teaspoon salt
	Fresh ground pepper to taste

Clean the squid and slice into rings, but keep the tentacles whole.

Put the oil into a heated sauté pan, add the garlic and onions, then cook until they are clear. Add the tomatoes and seasonings, then gently simmer for 10 minutes.

Drain the squid of excess water and add to the simmering tomato mixture. Maintain medium heat and stir periodically as the temperature rises. Once the mixture resumes a gentle boil, set the timer for 5 minutes. Stir occasionally to ensure even cooking.

Serve immediately to prevent overcooking.

*See Kitchen Notes

For garlic toast rounds:

1 loaf French bread	*½ cup melted margarine or oil*
1 clove garlic, minced	*1 teaspoon parsley, chopped*

Cut the bread into 1-inch slices and toast both sides lightly under the broiler. Mix together the melted butter, garlic, and parsley, then spread onto toast rounds and heat until the butter bubbles.

Shrimp & Clams
with Linguine

Serves 2

1 dozen littleneck clams, rinsed well
1 dozen medium shrimp, uncooked, peeled, and deveined
1 large tomato, sliced into thin wedges
2 scallions, cut into ¼-inch lengths
1 clove of garlic, minced
2 tablespoons olive oil
¼ cup white wine
6 ounces of fresh linguine

Bring 2 quarts of water to a boil in a medium saucepan for the pasta, then keep this hot while you prepare the clams and shrimp.

Rinse the clams well. Peel and devein the shrimp.

Pour the olive oil into a heated 10-inch skillet, add the garlic, and cook on medium heat for 2 or 3 minutes. Add in the whole clams with 1 cup of water, cover the pan, and turn the heat on high.

Cook the linguine according to package directions, which usually takes 3 to 5 minutes in boiling water. Make sure the strands are separated well as you put them into the water.

Check the clams after they have been cooking for 5 minutes. They should have popped open in that time. If not, cover the pan and cook for another minute or two. Add the shrimp, tomatoes, scallions, and wine to the boiling broth. Cover and cook for 2 minutes, shaking the pan once or twice to ensure even cooking.

Fresh linguine cooks in less time than dry pasta. If you use dry pasta, begin cooking it as soon as this pasta water boils and before starting to cook the clams.

Test the linguine. If it is done, drain the water and hold the pasta hot until the shrimp and clams are ready. You may want to toss it with a little olive oil to keep it from sticking.

Divide the pasta into 2 portions on soup plates or in shallow bowls. Spoon the clams and shrimp onto each serving, then pour broth over it all. Serve with Parmesan cheese.

Shad Roe

Serves 2

WE THANK the late Dot Hoskins for her input on the preparation of this seasonal delicacy. As with all seafood, the key is not to overcook it!

4 pieces of bacon
2 sets of shad roe

In a medium skillet, cook the 4 pieces of bacon until crisp. Remove the bacon from the pan and allow the fat to cool only slightly before laying 2 sets of roe in the pan. Turn the sets over at once so they are coated with the bacon drippings. Cover the pan and cook on medium to low heat for 10 to 15 minutes, turning once.

Serve with the bacon and hot, parsleyed potatoes for a meal that has satisfied generations of shore dwellers!

Linguine
with White Clam Sauce

Serves 4 to 6

AS MENTIONED in preparing the Gourmet Pizza (*page 25*), this recipe can be made using all quahogs or a combination of half quahogs/half sea clams.

4 tablespoons olive oil	*1 pint clam juice*
3 cloves of garlic, chopped fine	*1 tablespoon fresh parsley, chopped*
1 cup chopped onion	*1 teaspoon basil*
½ pint chopped quahogs	*1 teaspoon oregano*
½ pint chopped sea clams	*Fresh ground black pepper to taste*

In a large skillet, heat the oil. Add the garlic and onion, then cook on medium until the onions are clear. Add the clams and cook for 5 minutes, stirring occasionally. Add the juice and herbs, then bring to a gentle boil.

If you won't be using the sauce right away, turn off the heat to prevent overcooking the clams and making them tough.

Following the directions on the package, cook the linguine until it is *al dente*. Add this to the sauce and simmer together for one or two minutes, allowing the pasta to absorb some of the liquid and a lot of the flavor. You may add a little extra water at this time to make more sauce.

Adjust the seasonings and serve immediately. Don't forget the Parmesan or Romano cheese!

Scrod San Sebastian

S CROD SAN SEBASTIAN is a perennial favorite at our restaurant. The dish was inspired by a meal we enjoyed in the town of the same name on the northern coast of Spain. There the original recipe was made with a steaked white fish. We have adapted it for the American palate which prefers to see the fish on the plate without its skin and bones. This makes a delightful meal when served with a crispy green salad and a loaf of crusty bread.

FOR EACH PERSON, ALLOW:
> *6 to 8 ounces fresh scrod or other white fish*
> *3 or 4 littleneck clams, rinsed well*
> *2 teaspoons butter or margarine*
> *¼ teaspoon chopped garlic*
> *¼ cup water*
> *2 teaspoons scallions, chopped*
> *1 teaspoon parsley, chopped*

Because the fish fillets are somewhat delicate, it is best not to prepare a large quantity in one pan. A serving for 4 should be the maximum in a 10-inch pan. If you are making 5 to 8 servings, use two frying pans at once and arrange the seafood so it is only one layer deep. By the same token, if you are making only 1 or 2 servings, use a small enough pan so that the fish simmers in the juices.

Begin by heating a frying pan of appropriate size, adding the oil, then the garlic, and cooking briefly. Add the remaining ingredients in the order listed, making certain to snuggle the clams (hinge-side down) in around the fish pieces. Cover and cook on medium heat until the clams are all open. Depending on the quantities, this should be about 10 to 15 minutes.

Taking care that the fish pieces don't fall apart, use a spoon or spatula to transfer the fish and the clams either to a serving dish, or to individual dishes. Pour the liquid over the rest and serve.

Fillet of Sole
with Shitake Champagne Sauce

Serves 6

THIS DELICATE ENTRÉE is easy on the cook *and* the palate!

3 pounds fillet of sole

FOR THE SAUCE:

4 ounces shitake mushrooms   *3 tablespoons flour*
¾ cups champagne   *Dash white pepper*
1½ cups fish stock, heated   *1 tablespoon fresh chopped chives*
2 tablespoons butter

Rinse the mushrooms well, then remove the stems and slice the caps.

In a small saucepan, combine the champagne, the mushroom stems, and half the mushroom caps. Bring to a boil, then reduce heat and allow the mushrooms to simmer for 10 minutes. Drain off the champagne and add it to the heated stock. Set the mushrooms aside.

In a medium sauté pan, melt the butter, add the uncooked mushrooms, then stir for 5 minutes or until the pieces are quite limp. Sprinkle the flour into the pan and cook for another minute before adding the stock. As you add the stock, stir well to eliminate lumps.

Add the cooked mushrooms, then turn the heat to a low setting and simmer gently for 10 minutes, stirring frequently.

Preheat oven to 400° F Butter a shallow baking dish and arrange the fish in it. If the fillets are small, overlap 2 or 3 pieces of fish to form four portions. Cover the dish with foil or a lid and bake for 15 minutes; 20 minutes, if you have used a glass or earthenware dish.

When the fish is done, remove to individual plates and pour the cooking liquid into the sauce.

Ladle sauce over each serving, sprinkle with chopped chives and serve.

Baked Whitefish
with Herbs & Vegetables

Serves 4

HEART HEALTHY and easy to prepare, this dish is cooked in the oven in its own juices. With no added oils or carbohydrates you could eat two portions and still have a clear conscience!

2 pounds whitefish fillets (such as whiting, hake, cusk, tilapia, cod, haddock, or pollock)

¼ cup scallions, sliced
½ cup shallots, diced
½ cup celery (include leaves), sliced
1 tablespoon fresh thyme, chopped
2 tablespoons sundried tomatoes, chopped
½ cup water
1 carrot, julienned
2 teaspoons lemon zest
3 tablespoons parsley, chopped
Salt & pepper to taste

Refresh the sundried tomatoes by soaking them in hot water for 10 minutes.

Select a shallow baking dish just big enough to contain the fish. Spread the vegetables and herbs on the bottom, reserving 1 tablespoon of herb mix for the top.

Add the water, then lay the fish over the vegetables. Season with salt and pepper, then sprinkle with the lemon zest, sundried tomatoes, and remaining herbs.

Cover and bake in a preheated 400° F oven for 20 minutes or until the fish flakes easily with a fork.

Coho Salmon
with Rice Stuffing

Serves 4

THIS RICE STUFFING can also be used with trout.

4 coho salmon, whole, dressed; about 12 ounces each

1 cup uncooked rice	*1 tablespoon fresh chopped dill*
1 teaspoon salt	*2 teaspoons lemon juice*
2 shallots, minced	*2 tablespoons white wine*
1 cup sliced mushrooms	*1 tablespoon Worcestershire sauce*
2 tablespoons butter	*¼ teaspoon white pepper*
1 tablespoon flour	

Cook the rice in 2 cups of water to which the salt has been added.

Meanwhile, heat a sauté pan, melt the butter, and add in the shallots and mushrooms. Cook until shallots are clear and mushrooms are tender. Sprinkle the flour into the pan and cook for a minute.

Combine the lemon juice, Worcestershire sauce, wine and white pepper. Pour the mix into the pan and cook for 2 or 3 minutes, stirring well.

Add the mushroom mix and dill into the cooked rice, stirring to combine all the ingredients.

In a shallow bowl or a pie plate, mix 1 cup flour with 1 teaspoon salt, 1 teaspoon paprika, and ½ teaspoon black pepper. Dredge the fish in the flour (skin side only) and lay them on their sides in a buttered baking dish.

Divide the stuffing evenly among the fish, placing it on the bottom half so you can bring the other half over the top. Try to cover most of the stuffing so it won't dry out during baking.

Preheat oven to 400° F.

Bake, uncovered, for 20 minutes. Check to be sure it is done. If additional cooking is required, you may want to cover the fish lightly with foil to prevent drying.

The Summer Catch

ORIGINALLY ONLY A SEASONAL MARKET catering to the summer trade, Swan River Fish Market was born in summertime, when the population increases ten times that of the locals throughout Cape Cod, Nantucket & Martha's Vineyard. Then it took some forty years to work up the nerve to remain open on a year-round basis.

Coincidentally, the fresh seafood selection increases tremendously during summer as well. Striped bass, bluefish, tuna, swordfish, lobsters (inshore), shark, and eels are among the many delights that begin to surface in our market during those weeks, and we decide upon the catch of the day for our restaurant only after seeing what the fishermen arrive with off the boat that morning. Truly, the meal is the catch of the day.

Clearly, then, summer is a season of plenty: of fresh fish, of people, and of work! But it gets our juices running, and it's really plenty of fun.

The first bluefish we see of the season are taken out of the weir traps in Nantucket Sound. By then, sport fishermen who really know their stuff have already been catching them for a month. The early hot spots are on the south sides of the islands of Nantucket and Martha's Vineyard, as well as off Popponesset Beach in Mashpee. These first bluefish to arrive are called "racers". Generally full-grown, adult fish, they are thin and scrawny from their long journey.

A true gamefish, blues often are caught by anglers who just love to catch fish, not eat them. Left in the sun for any time at all and improp-

The fresh seafood selection increases during summer. Striped bass, tuna, bluefish, swordfish, lobsters, shark, and eels are among the delights that surface in our market during those weeks.

erly handled, their catch is easily ruined. So, we turn away such fish all summer. In fact, those weekend warriors in their boat-toys who literally destroy schools of bluefish are the bane of real fishermen.

Bluefish aside, striped bass are the premier gamefish to inhabit Cape & Islands waters. Stripers are regarded as highly for their difficulty to catch, as they are for their fine taste. Now added to the striped bass eminent stature is their legendary comeback.

Five years ago, the species was on the verge of extinction. Like many of our fish resources, they were overfished, polluted out of their spawning grounds, and nearly wiped out of their ocean habitat altogether. But through fishing conservation laws put into effect along the eastern seaboard, bass have made a terrific rebound. A few years ago, there were so few bright spots for wild fish lovers to look at with so many fish resources at all-time lows; however, striped bass and many other fish are proving that – with proper efforts – the oceans can be managed and harvested to feed a hungry world.

Massachusetts law allows only a set quota of stripers to be caught for commercial sale beginning on the first of July. All commercial fishermen must have permits, and a striped bass must measure nearly 36 inches in length to be a "keeper". This has been the law since 1991. All states along the eastern seaboard which have stripers also have strict management plans in effect. Striped bass stocks are now considered to be at historic levels; never have more fish been known to exist throughout their range. Long after the commercial season for catching striped bass has ended, tremendous numbers of stripers are still sighted basking in warm waters around Cape Cod, Nantucket & Martha's Vineyard.

Yet another interesting summer arrival to Cape & Islands waters is shark, which were ignored by most fishermen for many years. I first saw people eating them when I was attempting to support the family as a commercial fisherman in the Florida Keys. Until then, I had thought it was only the other way around: shark eats man.

In Florida, sharks were a constant problem when I was fishing for king mackerel. All too often I would pull in my catch, only to see a blue

Striped bass and many other fish are proving that – with proper efforts – the oceans can be managed and harvested to feed a hungry world.

or a hammerhead shark take it from me at the side of the boat. Once they had found our fishing spot, we would have to move on, leaving behind our huge school of mackerel. Any time we caught a black-tip or a lemon shark, though, that fish was destined for the grill.

In our northern waters, mako is the best shark for flavor. Cecy and I first featured mako on our Swan River menu twenty years ago, when it was a novelty, and people were full of both questions and doubt. That's no longer the case, however, and now even mako are overfished and regulated. So, we list it on the menu as when available. Sharks are one of the slowest growing fish in the sea, so their increasing popularity has led to their scarcity. Perhaps new fishing regulations will allow mako to re-bound as stripers did.

Dreaded by our cod fishermen, sand sharks (also known as "dogfish", "Cape dogfish", etc.) are also extremely abundant in summer. When the dogs show up, many a cod fisherman has been known to haul in his gear and head for shore. Historically, dogfish has had little or no commercial value, and their numbers make other fish difficult to catch.

In the past decade, however, dogfish has become a targeted species around our waters. With cod, haddock, and flounder so hard to find, the market for dogfish has opened up considerably. Still, 90 per cent of the catch is shipped out of the country, where much of it ends up being served as fish & chips in England. While it is an excellent tasting fish, dogfish remains very difficult to process. Unfortunately, we are not able to take advantage of this resource, and we just watch it get boxed up and trucked off-Cape. Dogfish are now considered by the Federal govern-ment to be an over-fished species, and they are now protected by law. This has not gone over well with the local fishermen who can't harvest cod, because the dogs are so prevalent in local waters.

One of the grandest fish in the sea must be halibut, which are caught in cold water oceans throughout many parts of the world. While halibut used to be very plentiful on Georges Bank, some 75 miles east of Nan-tucket, catching a local halibut now is like finding gold.

I can remember unloading halibut by the dozens at the Chatham fish

One of the grand-est fish in the sea must be halibut, which are caught in cold water oceans through-out many parts of the world.

pier thirty years ago, where each year a fish buyer from New York's Fulton Market would offer a $100 bonus to the Chatham fisherman who caught the largest halibut during the month of May. So, that wise old fishmonger ended up with some of the largest, freshest halibut along the eastern seaboard. Unfortunately, no undersize limit then existed for halibut. Today, a solitary halibut landing turns many a head on the dock.

Tuna are among our most spectacular summer visitors. In years past, the only people we knew who ate fresh tuna were either adventurous fishermen, or else travelers from the Mediterranean or Asia. In fact, when I first was introduced to fresh tuna, I was told it had to be soaked overnight in milk or marinade to make it palatable. Wow, what a waste! As we now know, fresh tuna, grilled quickly, then topped with a nice salsa or sauce can be as satisfying as any steak.

Carefully monitored and regulated now, tuna can be caught only by fishermen who have a special permit. The fish is individually tagged, and the buyer must log all catches for weekly reporting to the state and federal governments. When the annual quota is reached for each type (bluefin, big-eye, yellowfin, etc.), then fishing is closed until the next year. Nothing is harder for a captain to do in September than to head for the fishing grounds as tuna leap all around and know that the season is closed. He can look, but he cannot touch. And when one tuna might be worth $15,000 on the Japanese market, it's better for him to not even look!

Rod-and-reel tuna fishing is one of the nicest jobs Ive ever observed. Oh, yes, it's risky and often unproductive. And it involves an initial investment of tens of thousands of dollars, as well as a ton of experience. I had the great fortune of going aboard a commercial boat out of Harwichport with Captain Pat Hynes a couple of years back, and what a life! You steam out of port for an hour or two. You stop, set your trolls at your favorite spot, then sit back and wait. And watch.

The beauty of the day is only part of the job. Tuna are generally found in the same feeding areas as whales and dolphins. So, while you wait for the fussy tuna to consider striking your lure, you are treated to a show that whale-watching boats all pray for. While not a single tuna

In years past, the only people we knew who ate fresh tuna were some adventurous fishermen, or else travelers from the Mediterranean or Asia.

might ever strike your bait, dozens of whales and porpoises are likely to play all day. In fact, most boats have more empty-handed trips than productive ones, but what a great day at the office!

The fish that probably give me the greatest optimism are salmon. Twenty years ago they were almost unheard of, except in summer: salmon and peas on the 4th of July, one of the classic fish-holidays. I never realized this, however, until I worked in a fish market during that time of year. During June, we would be selling fifty pounds of salmon a week; then Mr. Folsom, my first fish-mentor, would order 300 or 400 pounds for the first week of July! And we never seemed to have enough.

Back then, salmon were flown in from Alaska and the Pacific Northwest, but we would acquire some higher-priced Atlantic salmon for our fussiest customers. Though Atlantic salmon range from the Gulf of Maine to Nova Scotia, the stock was so low that the fishery all but ended.

Today salmon have become the premier farmed, or aquacultured fish in the world. Norway was the first country to develop farm-raised production, Great Britain, Chile, and Canada all followed closely behind. So successful were their efforts that too many fish were brought to market and prices collapsed. Buying Salmon became a United Nations experience, and we have benefited from this development. Small salmon farms now are found close enough to us that we can simply call the farmer and order fish for the next day. They are of superior quality, as fresh as any fish our boats are bringing in.

Salmon aquaculture has proven that seafood has a future. Many other types of fish and shellfish are also being farm-raised successfully, including local mussels, oysters, and quahogs. Not only does this guarantee us high quality seafood, but also it reduces pressure on wild stocks, thus improving the outlook for our local fishermen.

While we're on the topic of local shellfish, this season seems to be a natural time to enjoy all kinds. So natural, in fact, that you wonder whether our shellfishermen should really get paid during summer. Just look where they work: along the beach, on sandbars that pop-up at low tide, in meandering rivers on quiet mornings, where they are joined only

Salmon aquaculture has proven that seafood has a future. Many other types of fish and shellfish are also being farm-raised successfully, including local mussels, oysters and quahogs.

by gulls, geese, terns, and blue herons. Their biggest occupational hazards are greenhead flies and sunburns. Then they come into the market with their cut-off shorts, four-wheel drives, and maybe a cold beer to quench their thirst. For this they get paid? Yes, they demand money for what they've just plucked from the wild! (Sorry, I couldn't resist a joke from one of my favorite fishcutters, Franny Coe. The last thing any fisherman wants to hear is: "Why are you complaining about the price we are paying you? You got them for nothing?") I know from experience how hard they do work for those clams.

Shellfish are easier to harvest in the summertime, because all the different types of clams rise closer to the surface during warm weather. The seas are generally calmer as well. One hazard that increases in summer, however, is pollution. With greater numbers of people, boats, and seabirds comes greater numbers of pollutants. As in most states, clean water monitoring has increased tremendously in Massachusetts during the past thirty years. We are required to follow strict guidelines, known as the "Shellfish Traceability Program," which works to protect your health.

Any waterway which is open to commercial shellfishing must be tested constantly, and our fishermen must identify specifically where they obtained their shellfish. We must document this, including a tag which must travel with the shellfish to the fish market, the restaurant, or wherever it is destined. That tag must be kept for 90 days after the shellfish is consumed, so any problems can be easily traced to the source. If you buy shellfish from a dealer you know and trust, you are quite safe in eating shellfish, raw or cooked. Of course, this doesn't make good copy for the media, so don't expect to hear about it from them. In fact, as of the latest Federal Food Code law, all restaurants in the United States must have warnings on their menus advising customers of the risks of eating raw or undercooked clams, oysters, steak, eggs, et cetera. It makes me wonder when I travel overseas why anyone is still alive without such government protection.

Shellfish are tricky to handle properly, and mishandling does occur out there. Storage, rotation, temperature, cleanliness all are very impor-

If you buy shellfish from a dealer you know and trust, you are quite safe in eating shellfish, raw or cooked.

tant. But if you purchase shellfish from a reputable dealer, the delight of fresh shellfish is not a thing of the past.

Steamers are one of the best and most abundant shellfish on the Cape & Islands. But what do you do about the sand? When I was a boy, my family always summered in Maine, where I remember the first time digging clams in some wonderful, soft, black mud, somewhere near Bar Harbor. What a joyous discovery! But there was no sand to worry about. No grit. No crunch. Not at all like steamers around Cape Cod, Nantucket & Martha's Vineyard. When I finally dug clams from these waters I realized why. The clams live in sand, not mud! Simple, huh?

So how do you get the sand out of our clams? I love to hear all the methods that people boast of knowing. Its almost like hiccup cures. They all sound great. Some work some of the time. The best one is to put pepper on them, and they will sneeze the sand out. I refuse to tell you that my method is the right one. I'll just tell you what we do. We take cold tap water, add a small amount of salt, and agitate the mix. Then we put the clams in and keep them in a cooler for two to three hours. Occasionally, we swirl them around a bit. If clams are left in water too long, they drown from lack of oxygen. But the key to not eating sand with your clam comes after it is cooked. Any sand left is generally at the base of the "foot" or neck of the mollusk. I recommend turning that part inside out and swirling it well in the hot clam broth before dipping it in the buter. If you do find any remaining sand when you are eating, just remember what my Nana always said: "You've got to eat a peck of dirt before you die." I never figured out why.

The Cape & Islands benefit from an abundant resource of quahogs, those hardshell clams known in the marketplace as "littlenecks", "cherrystones", and "chowder clams". Though they are found all the way down to Florida, a coldwater quahog (meatier, saltier, and cleaner-tasting) far outshines any clam I've tasted from Southern waters.

Digging quahogs is one of the most satisfying times I've spent at the shore. While sunbathing on a beach never appealed to me, not everyone sees the virtues in scratching for clams. You have to go out in wader boots

The key to not eating sand with your clam comes after it is cooked.

two hours before low tide to stand in water about three feet deep. And there you harvest nature's garden with a four-pronged rake. Each time you strike a clam, you hear a *ping*. (A *pong* is only a rock!) You pull the quahog out of its muddy bed, measure it for legal size, then either keep it, or toss it back. Scratching the right spot for two hours on either side of low tide, a real quahogger can make a day's pay.

Bullraking is another method of quahogging. This is done from a boat at high tide. The bullrake is a 30-foot aluminum extension rake, which requires the strength of a . . . (You guessed it!) Fortunately, both of these ancient forms of shellfishing are still in common practice on the Cape & Islands today. Although aquaculture is on the increase, most of the clams we sell are still a product of the wild.

Conch is most commonly associated with the Caribbean, so not many people realize that Nantucket Sound and many of the rivers and bays throughout this area are loaded with this shellfish. While our recipe for conch chowder is derived from many tastings in the Florida Keys, anyone eating the dish down there is eating conch meat from the Philippines or the Bahamas. In local waters, though, we are able to harvest conch throughout the year, where they are a bountiful food source. Still, conchs are considered a nuisance. They devour other shellfish, such as scallops and clams, and they are not a joy to clean, but they are a good food source.

Mussels are another example of one person's trash being another's treasure. How could mussels have gone unnoticed throughout these parts for so long? Of course, we all knew they were there. For years, we would run aground on islands of them at low tide, and all the sea ducks and gulls would feast on them. For years, there was little or no market for them. No longer. The word is out, and the mussels supply is being depleted.

The legal limit for a day's catch of mussels in Chatham was 200 bushels. Boat after boat would land with their limit. Now the mussel resource in Chatham is almost gone. Heavy fishing, shifting sands, and voracious birds all have contributed to their demise. Fortunately, several

Mussels are an example of one person's trash being another's treasure. How could mussels have gone so long without notice throughout these parts?

local fishermen have successful mussel farms working in areas like Pleasant Bay and Town Cove in Orleans, as well as various spots in Eastham and Provincetown. Mussels grow fast, and they multiply quickly. All they need is clean, cold water, and proper management.

Mussels are the shellfish of the people. Long appreciated by French chefs, more recently they have been endorsed by Americans. A generous serving can still be bought for a dollar. Whether they are on the menu at our house or not, I can't resist scooping a handful whenever I'm kayaking around Morris Island in Chatham. (Of course, I do have a Chatham shellfish license. Don't leave home without it.)

Lobsters are a large part of our world throughout the Cape & Islands. It's funny, but whenever I travel to Florida or the West Coast or even the Caribbean, North Atlantic Lobsters are referred to as "Maine lobsters". At least half of our first-time customers think that our lobsters must come from Maine; however, hundreds of thousands of pounds of lobsters are brought into port from our local waters. In fact, America's lobster fishery began here during the early 19th Century, and the nation's first and only lobster hatchery remains on the Vineyard.

With ports from Sandwich to Provincetown, Cape Cod Bay is loaded with lobster pots all summer long. Most of the lobsters caught in Cape Cod Bay, though, are small, "chicken lobsters" that run up to 1½ pounds each. The bay has a migratory lobster population, so few lobsters are found there in winter or spring, and most are caught from late spring through late fall.

While Nantucket Sound also has a large lobster population, the majority of our lobsters are caught east of Chatham: The Great Backside of the Cape. The lobsters caught by our Chatham and Orleans boats are generally larger than those out of Cape Cod Bay. All lobsters molt or shed their shells, once or twice a year. When they are soft-shelled, they hibernate without eating. Consequently, when you open the shell you find very little meat. A 1-pound hardshell lobster has 4 ounces of meat; however, the same size softshell lobster yields only 2 to 3 ounces of meat.

All summer long, when Maine is full of softshell shedders, our

America's lobster fishery began on the Cape & Islands during the early 19th Century, and the nation's first and only lobster hatchery remains on the Vineyard.

Chatham run is rock hard. I'll never forget one of our lobstermen unloading his catch into our tank. One of the customers asked if our lobsters were hardshells. Bill just took out a nice 3-pounder, put it on the concrete floor, then stood on the claw. All 240 pounds of him. The claw didn't give a bit, which told the customer all he wanted to know.

Lobstering would seem to be a fishery that is in decent shape. For years, there have been limits to the number of licenses in Massachusetts, there have been limits to the number of pots allowed per license, and data has been monitored to help manage this fishery. If such methods were applied to other fisheries thirty years ago, our cod and haddock stocks would not have declined so severely in the '80s and '90s.

When our tanks are full, we know it's summertime. We have two separate lobster holding systems that can hold about two tons of lobsters altogether. While it is not unusual to see one lobsterman catch 300 or 400 pounds of lobster in one day, lobstering is extremely hard work, and it can be dangerous. Two years ago one of our lobstermen, Tony Cocorro, was steaming home from loberstering. His son was at the helm while he washed down the deck. As he leaned over to gather a bucket of water, the boat rolled on a wave and over he went. His son never heard him. A half hour later, the boy looked around and realized what had happened. He put in a distress call to the Coast Guard, alerted other boats, and fretfully began searching the pitching seas for his father. Two hours later, defying all the laws of hypothermia, Tony was pulled from the 45° water still cussing. The only thing that kept him afloat was his washdown bucket he kept filled with air for floatation. He swore he would make it to land that he could see, even though the water was a hundred feet deep. A Coast Guardsman said that Tony never should have survived in that water after that long. No survival suit. No life jacket. They never expected a live recovery. The moral of that story is: never doubt the determination of a Cape Cod fisherman. And, yes, Tony is out there today, still fishing.

The moral of this story is: never doubt the determination of a Cape fisherman.

A Summer Menu

Appetizer
Mussels Diablo
Marinated Mussels
Three-Layer Seafood Terrine
Crabmeat Cocktail with Dijon Sauce
Crabmeat Spread on Toast Rounds
Smoked Fish Spread

Soup
Key West Conch Chowder

Salad
Seafood Pasta Salad
Calamari Salad
Swan River Shrimp Salad
Shrimp & Bowtie Pasta Salad
Grilled Fish Caesar Salad
Chilled Grilled Shrimp on Greens

Entrées
L.O.B. Grilled Fish
Chilled Poached Halibut with Dijon Sauce
Oriental Steamed Salmon
Blackened Salmon

Striped Bass in Filo with Red Pepper Mayonnaise
Grilled Swordfish
Seafood en Brochette
Grilled Yellowfin Tuna with Tomato Mint Sauce
Grilled Fresh Tuna with Rosemary Lime Marinade
Grilled Striped Bass with Fresh Fruit Salsa
Mako Shark Steak au Poivre
Bluefish Packets
Grilled Mahi-Mahi with Black Bean Salsa
Grilled Grouper en Brochette
Grilled Salmon Noisettes with Orange Mint Salsa
Salmon Baked in Parchment
Lobsters: Grilled or Broiled
New England Clambake
Kitchen Clambake

Mussels Diablo

Serves 4 to 6

SPICY HOT, but served chilled, this dish can easily be prepared ahead and presented as either a first course, or a luncheon salad on a bed of lettuce!

*4 pounds of mussels in the shell**

FOR THE MARINADE:

1 cup white wine	*2 tablespoons pimentos, sliced*
½ cup vinegar	*1 lemon, sliced thin*
1½ cup oil	*1 clove of garlic, chopped fine*
4 jalapeño peppers,	*1 teaspoon red pepper flakes*
sliced thin	*1 small Bermuda onion, thin wedges*

Clean the mussels well and remove the beards. In a large pot with 1 cup of water, steam the mussels about 10 minutes until all the shells are open. Drain off the broth and freeze for use in seafood soups or sauces.

Arrange a single layer of mussels in a shallow pan and refrigerate them while you prepare the marinade.

Mix together all the marinade ingredients except the oil. Add the oil, pouring in a slow steady stream, whisking continuously until it is blended well.

Once the mussels are chilled, put them into a glass dish and pour the marinade over them, stirring to be sure they are coated.

Refrigerate for at least 2 hours, stirring occasionally.

*See Kitchen Notes

Marinated Mussels

Serves 4 to 6

*4 pounds of mussels**

FOR THE MARINADE:
1 small Bermuda onion, cut into thin wedges
¼ cup white wine   1 tablespoon sugar
¼ cup red wine vinegar   1 teaspoon salt
¼ teaspoon thyme   Pinch of white pepper
¼ teaspoon basil   1½ cups oil
¼ teaspoon oregano   2 cloves garlic, minced

In a large pot with 1 cup of water, steam mussels for about 10 minutes, or until all the shells are open. Cool them and remove the meats from the shells. Refrigerate until needed.

Mix together all the marinade ingredients except the oil. Add the oil in a slow, steady stream, whisking continuously until it is blended well.

In a glass bowl, combine the mussels and marinade, stirring to coat all the meats.

Chill for at least 2 hours, stirring periodically to ensure that the mussels will be evenly marinated.

*See Kitchen Notes

Crabmeat Cocktail
with Dijon Sauce

W E LOVE CRABMEAT when it is *ultra* fresh, just out of the shell, well-chilled, and served with a Dijon sauce for dipping. Simply delicious!

FOR EACH PERSON, ALLOW:
> *4 ounces of fresh crabmeat*

FOR THE SAUCE:
> *Equal parts Dijon mustard and mayonnaise, using 2 tablespoons of each per person*

Using a small plate for each person, arrange the crabmeat on a red lettuce leaf, set a generous dollop of sauce alongside the meat and garnish each with a thin lemon wedge.

Crabmeat Spread
on Toast Rounds

Serves 6 to 8

1 loaf of French bread (2 or 3 inches in diameter is best)
8 ounces of fresh crabmeat   ½ teaspoon mustard powder
1 cup mayonnaise   Dash of garlic powder
2 tablespoons scallions, chopped   2 drops of Tabasco
½ cup Parmesan cheese   1½ teaspoons Worcestershire
                                    sauce

Cut the French bread into 1-inch slices and lightly toast both sides under the broiler. Set aside.

Blend the mustard powder and garlic powder into the Parmesan cheese. Mix this cheese mixture together with the mayonnaise, Worcestershire sauce and Tabasco.

Taking care not to break up all the chunks, gently fold in the drained crabmeat.

Just before serving, spread the crabmeat mix on the toast rounds. Sprinkle with Parmesan cheese and heat under the broiler until lightly browned. Serve at once.

Smoked Fish Spread

Makes 4 cups

A REFRESHING BLEND for a summer gathering. Keep it simple, garnish with lime wedges and serve with Saltines.

1 pound smoked fish, crumbled into small pieces

1 cup mayonnaise   *¾ teaspoon onion powder*
1 cup sour cream   *¾ teaspoon garlic powder*
1 teaspoon Tabasco   *¾ teaspoon celery salt*
1 tablespoon lime juice   *¾ teaspoon Old Bay seasoning*
1 tablespoon horseradish

Mix ingredients together and allow to sit for at least several hours before serving.

Three-Layer Seafood Terrine

T HIS RECIPE makes an elegant item for the buffet table, or can be
sliced and served on a bed of greens at the table.

Ingredients for each layer will be given first; instructions for making
the mousse, assembling the loaf, then cooking will follow. You will need
a 9 by 5 loaf pan.

FOR THE WHITE LAYER:

6 ounces whitefish (sole, haddock, or cod)

¼ teaspoon salt	*2 ounces feta cheese*
pinch white pepper	*½ egg**
pinch cayenne pepper	*½ cup heavy cream*

** Break 2 eggs into a cup and mix well with a fork. Use 1½ tablespoons
of mixed egg for each recipe.*

FOR THE GREEN LAYER:

6 ounces white fish (sole, haddock or cod)

*2 cups fresh spinach, stems removed, rinsed and firmly packed***

1 teaspoon fresh chopped dill	*pinch nutmeg*
¼ teaspoon salt	*½ egg**
pinch white pepper	*½ cup heavy cream*

*** The spinach must be steamed until quite limp, then drained well.
Squeeze it to remove any additional moisture.*

FOR THE PINK LAYER:

6 ounces salmon
2 tablespoons chopped pimento
¼ teaspoon salt
½ egg*
½ cup heavy cream
pinch of white pepper

TO MAKE THE MOUSSE:

Proceed as follows for each of the three different colors. Plan to clean the your food processor or blender well between each recipe to keep the colors separate.

Cut the fish into 1-inch chunks and put it into the food processor or blender with its respective seasonings, along with the spinach, cheese or pimento. Process until the fish is well ground, stopping once or twice to scrape down the sides of the bowl.

Add in the egg and mix again until it is incorporated.

Add in the cream while the machine is running, stopping a few times to be sure it is evenly mixed.

Once the mousse is well blended, remove to a small bowl, cover and refrigerate until all the colors are made.

TO COOK THE TERRINE:

Preheat the oven to 350° F.

Put the loaf pan in the freezer for a few minutes to chill it.

Brush the pan with olive oil and lay in the mousse beginning with pink, then white, then green. Smooth each layer carefully.

Brush a piece of foil, (10-by-6) with olive oil and place it directly on top of the mousse.

Place the loaf pan into another pan, pour 2 or 3 inches of water into the second pan, and put them both into the oven.

Bake for 1 hour or until the internal temperature is 140° F. Leave the terrine in the oven with the temperature turned off for anther half hour.

Cool at room temperature, then place the terrine in the refrigerator to chill completely.

Run a knife around the outer edge of the pan to loosen the mousse, then invert it carefully onto a plate.

Tips for making mousse:
- Keep all the ingredients, the bowls, and the utensils cold;
- Don't overwork the mixture;
- Use fresh fish, not frozen;
- Check fish for bones; remove discolored parts.

Garnish and serve well-chilled with a mayonnaise-based sauce, such as a scallion remoulade, cajun remoulade, or a red pepper mayonnaise.

Offer mild crackers (such as water crackers), toast points, or melba toast.

Key West Conch Chowder

WHO NEEDS TO TRAVEL to the southernmost outpost of Florida when you can prepare this Caribbean favorite with conch from our own local waters?

FOR A CHOWDER THAT SERVES 6 TO 8 PERSONS:

2 tablespoons olive oil
2 cloves of garlic, minced fine
1 large onion, diced
½ green pepper, diced
1 stalk of celery, diced
2 cups water
2 cups clam broth or fish stock
1 pound ground conch meat
1 cup crushed tomatoes
2 potatoes: peeled, diced and cooked al dente

2 tablespoons sherry
½ teaspoon Tabasco
1 teaspoon thyme
1 tablespoon fresh parsley, chopped
½ teaspoon red pepper flakes
2 tablespoons lime juice
1 tablespoon tomato paste
Pinch of white pepper

TO PREPARE THE CHOWDER:

Heat the olive oil in a large saucepan, then add the garlic, onion, green pepper, and celery. When the onions are clear, add the remaining ingredients and bring to the boiling point. Reduce the heat and simmer for an hour.

If the chowder becomes too thick, you may wish to add more water.

Seafood Pasta Salad

Serves 6 to 8

½ pound salmon fillet   *¼ pound scallops*
¼ pound cooked shrimp, sliced down the middle
¼ pound lobster meat, cut into small pieces (about ½-inch across)

1 cup mixed vegetables, julienned and lightly steamed. Broccoli, carrots,celery, green and red peppers are all good in this salad.

8 ounces medium macaroni shells 10 black olives, sliced
1 scallion, sliced fine   ½ Bermuda onion, thin wedges
1 tomato, in thin wedges   1 tablespoon chopped parsley
4 tablespoons Parmesan cheese

FOR THE VINAIGRETTE:
1 cup oil   *1 clove chopped garlic*
½ cup vinegar   *1 tablespoon sugar*
1 teaspoon basil   *Dash of Tabasco*
1 teaspoon oregano   *Salt & fresh ground black pepper
                            to taste*

TO PREPARE THE SALAD:

Cook the pasta until it is *al dente*, then drain and cool.

Steam the salmon and scallops in a small, covered saute pan with ½ cup of water for 10 minutes, then check the thickest part of the salmon to be sure it is cooked. The flesh should be light in color and flake easily with a fork. Drain off the water and lift the fish and scallops out, leaving the skin in the pan.

Check the salmon for bones and remove them before breaking the fish into bite-sized chunks. If the scallops are large, you may want to cut them into quarters. Put the fish, pasta, vegetables and other ingredients into a glass dish. Refrigerate while making the vinaigrette.

To prepare the vinaigrette:

In a small bowl, mix together all ingredients for the vinaigrette, except the oil. Add the oil in a slow, steady stream, whisking continuously until it is blended well.

To complete the salad:

Pour the vinaigrette over the salad, stirring it carefully. Cover and refrigerate at least 2 hours, stirring two or three times to distribute the dressing evenly.

Serve chilled on a bed of greens.

Calamari Salad

Serves 6 as an appetizer, or 4 as an entrée

2 pounds cleaned squid*, diced
1 cucumber, peeled, halved, seeded & sliced
1 cup mushrooms, quartered
Parsley & lemon, for garnish

FOR THE POACHING LIQUID:

2 quarts of water
10 whole black peppercorns

1 lemon, cut into thin rings
2 cloves of garlic, peeled & crushed

FOR THE DRESSING:

¼ cup tarragon vinegar
1 tablespoon parsley, chopped
Dash of white pepper

1 clove of garlic, minced
½ teaspoon of salt
¾ cup olive oil

Place the water, lemon rings, peppercorns and garlic cloves in a large saucepan and bring it to a boil. Reduce to a simmer and add the squid, stirring to separate. Squid will turn a whitish-pink color and should be done after 45 seconds to a minute. Drain immediately in a colander and rinse well under cold water to stop the cooking. Spread the cooked calamari in a shallow dish, then remove the peppercorns, lemons and garlic. Refrigerate the squid until it is well-chilled.

In a small bowl, combine the vinegar, garlic, parsley, salt and pepper. Whisk in the olive oil until the dressing is well-blended.

Place the calamari in a salad bowl with the cucumber and mushrooms.

*See Kitchen Notes

Whisk the dressing and pour it over the combined ingredients. Mix well and season to taste.

Refrigerate for at least an hour, stirring once or twice.

Before serving, garnish with parsley sprigs and thin slices of lemon.

Swan River Shrimp Salad

Serves 6

OUR NAPLES CUSTOMERS can't get enough of this shrimp salad. It's absolutely great on a bulky roll or a bed of mixed greens.

2 pounds cooked shrimp	*1½ teaspoons black pepper*
¾ cup diced celery	*¼ teaspoon celery salt*
½ cup finely diced red onion	*¼ teaspoon Old Bay seasoning*
½ cup mayonnaise	*1 tablespoon fresh lemon juice*

Cut the shrimp or leave it whole, depending on your preference. Combine all ingredients in a bowl and mix well. Refrigerate until needed.

Shrimp & Bowtie Pasta Salad

Serves 6 as lunch portion or 4 as dinner

1 pound medium shrimp, uncooked, peeled and deveined*

4 cups bowtie pasta, uncooked
2 cups asparagus, in 1-inch lengths
2 tablespoons fresh basil, in fine strips
2 plum tomatoes, diced

¼ cup pine nuts
¼ cup grated Parmesan
Lettuce

FOR THE DRESSING:

¼ cup vinegar
¼ cup lemon juice
1 clove garlic, minced
½ teaspoon salt

¼ teaspoon fresh ground black pepper
½ teaspoon sugar
¾ cup olive oil

For a decorative effect, slice the shrimp down the center. They will form elegant curls as they cook.

In a medium saucepan, bring two quarts of water to a boil. Add in the shrimp and cook for a minute or two. Shrimp cook very quickly and are done when meat is white or pink throughout.

Drain off boiling water and rinse immediately with cold water to stop the cooking process. Refrigerate until you are ready to assemble the salad.

Cook the pasta according to package directions. The asparagus may be added in for the last 2 minutes of cooking. Drain, rinse and put into large bowl.

*See Kitchen Notes

Toast the pine nuts in a small sauté pan. They will need close attention to prevent burning. Cook on medium heat, stirring frequently. Remove to a plate to cool.

Meanwhile, make the dressing. Put all ingredients, except the oil, into a 2-cup measure. Using a wire whisk to blend as you go, pour the oil slowly into the cup and continue whisking until dressing is emulsified.

When the pine nuts have cooled, add them, along with the shrimp, tomato, basil and Parmesan cheese into the bowl. Pour the dressing over the salad and toss ingredients to be sure all are coated with the dressing. Serve on a bed of lettuce.

Grilled Fish Caesar Salad

Serves 4 to 6

A PIECE of grilled fish on a heaping plate of Caesar salad makes a very refreshing warm weather dish. No secret to our Naples customers; this is one of our most popular menu items!

Use tuna, swordfish, halibut, grouper, snapper, or large shrimp. For a different taste, use pan-blackened fish.

FOR EACH PERSON, ALLOW:

Allow 6-8 ounces of fish. See L.O.B. *recipe (page 93) for instructions on how to grill the fish.*

FOR THE SALAD:

8 cups sliced Romaine lettuce
1 cup croutons
Parmesan cheese, grated fresh

FOR THE DRESSING:

2 egg yolks　　　　　　　　*¼ teaspoon thyme*
1 teaspoon chopped garlic　*½ teaspoon fresh ground black pepper*
1 teaspoon anchovy paste　*1 teaspoon Worcestershire sauce*
¼ cup lemon juice　　　　 *¼ cup Parmesan cheese*
¼ cup vinegar　　　　　　 *1 cup olive oil*
¼ teaspoon basil

TO MAKE THE DRESSING:

Combine all ingredients, except oil, in blender. Process briefly just to mix. With motor running on low speed, add the oil in a slow steady stream. Process until dressing is well blended. Refrigerate until ready to use.

Have the Romaine rinsed, dried, cut and in a mixing bowl before cooking the fish. As fish is cooking, dress the salad, add in the croutons and mix. Place on individual plates and top with the fish as soon as it is done.

Garnish with freshly grated Parmesan cheese.

Serve with crusty French bread.

Chilled, Grilled Shrimp
On Greens

USING as few as two, or as many as six shrimp per person, you can make this salad as a lunch, side salad, or first course. You could also arrange the ingredients on a platter for a striking addition to a buffet table.

Shrimp: medium to large, peeled and deveined
Mixed baby greens or mesculun mix, 1 cup per person

1 tablespoon fresh chopped basil *1 ripe avocado*
1 tablespoon chopped scallions *Cherry or grape tomatoes*

FOR THE TARRAGON VINAIGRETTE:

1 teaspoon dried tarragon *¼ teaspoon white pepper*
½ cup cider vinegar *½ teaspoon sugar*
¼ teaspoon salt *1 cup salad oil*

For ease of handling, thread the shrimp onto skewers. Sprinkle with fresh lemon juice, brush with olive oil, then sprinkle with a little salt and pepper.

Cook them on the grill, only 2 or 3 minutes for each side if your grill is very hot. Grilling shrimp is an art so if you aren't sure whether they are done or not, make a small cut with a sharp knife into the thickest part of the shrimp. Cooked shrimp will be opaque white or pink all the way through. Keep in mind they will continue to cook a little even after they are removed from the heat, so don't hesitate to remove them if you think they're close to done. Allow the shrimp to cool, then refrigerate until needed.

To prepare the tarragon vinaigrette:

Put all dressing ingredients, except the oil, into a measuring cup. Stirring with a wire whisk as you go, pour the oil in a slow steady stream into the cup and continue whisking until dressing is well blended. Set aside until needed. (You may need to re-mix the dressing if the oil separates.)

Prepare the greens, mix with the basil and scallions, and set them onto the plates.

Arrange the shrimp, avocado slices, and tomatoes on top.

Drizzle each with dressing and serve.

L.O.B. Grilled Fish

Serves 4

LEMON, OIL, AND BASIL (L.O.B.) make a *very* useful concoction for the busy cook. The ingredients keep the preparation simple but really bring out the flavor of grilled fish. This combination is recommended for both northern and southern species.

2 pounds fish steak or fillet

FOR THE MARINADE:

½ cup lemon juice   *2 tablespoons finely chopped fresh parsley*
½ cup olive oil   *2 tablespoon finely chopped fresh basil*
½ teaspoon salt   *1 tablespoon minced garlic*
½ teaspoon ground black pepper

Mix marinade ingredients together. Set aside about a third of the fresh marinade to apply right before serving. One to two hours before you wish to cook, lay the fish into a glass dish and drizzle the marinade over it, coating both sides. Refrigerate until you are ready to cook .

When the grill is quite hot, place the fish on it and cook, turning once. Cooking time will depend on the thickness of the fish and the heat of the grill. (You may need to rearrange pieces as some parts of the grill will be hotter than others.)

Spoon or brush a little more lemon oil mix onto the fish in the very last minutes of cooking. Check for doneness.* Serve immediately.

*See Kitchen Notes

Chilled Poached Halibut
with Dijon Sauce

CHILLED SEAFOOD IS A DELIGHT in the summertime! The taste is refreshing, and it's easy on the cook. Poached halibut can be prepared in the morning, then served as a picnic lunch, or a formal evening meal.

FOR EACH PERSON, ALLOW:
> *Allow ½ pound of halibut*

FOR THE POACHING LIQUID:
> *3 cups of water*   *10 black peppercorns*
> *1 small bay leaf*   *2 lemons sliced into wedges*

In a 10-inch frying pan, combine the water, black peppercorns, bay leaf and lemon wedges (give them a little squeeze, then drop them in). Bring the water to a boil and add the halibut. The fish must be cooked gently to keep it tender and moist. Maintain a temperature just below the boiling point, cover the pan, and simmer for 10 minutes. To check for doneness, pierce the fish at the thickest part. If the flesh is opaque throughout, the fish is cooked and can be lifted out of the water with a slotted spoon or spatula. Place the fish on a plate, cover loosely, and refrigerate.

For each serving, use 2 tablespoons each of Dijon mustard and mayonnaise. Mix together well and chill.

When the fish is completely chilled, remove the skin and bones carefully, then arrange on a bed of lettuce. Serve the sauce in a small dish set beside the plate. Garnish with lemon and parsley.

Oriental Steamed Salmon

For each person, allow:

½ pound Atlantic salmon fillet

1 tablespoon each of carrot, ginger, and scallion cut into matchstick pieces 1-inch long
¼ cup each of teriyaki sauce and water

Cut the salmon into portions and place them in a frying pan of appropriate size. Top each piece with a mixture of the vegetables. In a measuring cup, mix equal parts teriyaki sauce and water, then pour into the pan, cover, and begin cooking over medium heat. Simmer gently for 10 minutes, then check for doneness.*

Remove the salmon carefully. Set each serving in a pool of the sauce on a small, warmed plate. Serve with a side dish of steaming rice.

*See Kitchen Notes

Blackened Salmon

WITH THE ACRID SMOKE from this method of cooking you need a good ventilation system, or else prepare it outdoors. In either case, avoid inhaling the smoke.

FOR EACH PERSON, ALLOW:
Allow ½ pound of Atlantic salmon steak or fillet per person
Pan-blackening spice (available at most supermarkets)

TO PREPARE THE MEAL INDOORS:
Preheat a cast iron frying pan for 10 minutes on the stovetop, using the highest possible heat. Preheat the oven to 400° F.

Coat both sides of the fish with pan-blackening spice. This mix is very spicy, so you'll probably prefer just a light sprinkle on your fish. For the full dose, spread the mix on a plate and lay the fish in it.

Put the fish into the pan and cook for 3 minutes on each side. Remove from the heat and check for doneness.* If the salmon needs more cooking, finish it in the oven.

TO PREPARE THE MEAL OUTDOORS:
Cook the seasoned fish on a hot grill for about 5 minutes per side, then check for doneness.*

*See Kitchen Notes

Striped Bass in Filo
with Red Pepper Mayonnaise

ROASTING RED PEPPER is best done on a gas flame or outside grill. To willfully char food goes against the grain of most reasonable cooks, yet we ask you to bear with us on this one because the resulting taste simply can't be beat!

FOR EACH PERSON, ALLOW:
> *Allow ½ pound of bass per person*

FOR THE MAYONNAISE:
> *1 egg yolk*　　　　　　*1 teaspoon lemon juice*
> *¼ teaspoon salt*　　　　*Dash white pepper*
> *Roasted red pepper*　　　*1 cup salad oil*

Using a long-handled fork, hold a red bell pepper over an open flame and thoroughly char the outer skin. Once it is all black, enclose it in an airtight container or plastic bag for an hour. Take the pepper out of the bag, immerse it in cold water, and rub the outer, blackened skin to remove it. Remove the seeds and membranes, then cut into medium chunks.

Put all the ingredients for the mayonnaise, except the oil, into a blender or food processor and process until the peppers are puréed. With the blender turned on, add the oil in a slow, steady stream, pausing once to scrape down the sides of the bowl. When the mixture looks like a light pink mayonnaise, it is done, and may be removed to a small bowl and refrigerated until needed.

Check the fish for bones by running your fingers lightly over the surface. Because bass bones usually are large and stubborn, you will probably need a pair of small pliers to remove them. Remove the skin and cut the fish into portion sizes. Refrigerate until needed.

Preheat the oven to 350° F.

Carefully unfold the filo dough onto a clean work space. Keep a clean, dampened kitchen towel handy to lay over the unused sheets in case you are interrupted, or they start to dry out while you are working. Peel off a sheet, lay it on the counter and brush it lightly with melted butter. Lay another sheet on top, brush and repeat.

Cut the three sheets in half widthwise. Set a piece of fish (skin side down) on the filo, about 3 inches from the end of the rectangle. Lift that 3-inch edge up to the fish, then roll the dough and fish over once. Pick up the flaps of dough on either side of the fish and fold them onto what is now the top.

Continue rolling the fish and dough, end over end, keeping the sides tucked in, until you run out of dough.

Place the packet, seam side down, onto a buttered cookie sheet, making sure that the edges are tucked in. Ideally, the fish itself will be skin side down. If not, try to adjust the original placement of the next piece onto the filo.

Wrap each piece of fish, then brush lightly with butter as you place them on the pan.

Bake for 20 to 25 minutes. Serve with a generous dollop of the red pepper mayonnaise on the side.

Grilled Swordfish

So SIMPLE TO PREPARE, this recipe is still one of the great tastes of summer!

FOR EACH PERSON, ALLOW:
Allow ½ pound of swordfish

To help retain the natural juices in swordfish and to keep it from sticking to the grill, lightly spread each side of the fish with mayonnaise. Depending on the intensity of heat, as well as the thickness of the fish, cook the swordfish for about 5 minutes on each side. To test for doneness, insert a thin, sharp knife into the flesh at the thickest point. If it meets with any resistance, the fish needs to cook longer. If the knife goes in like butter, the fish is done.

Seafood en Brochette

Serves 4

BROCHETTES TAKE A LITTLE TIME TO ASSEMBLE and should marinate for at least 2 hours. Once the preparation is complete, however, they are very easy to cook and serve.

FOR THE BROCHETTES:

1½ pounds of swordfish
¾ pound medium raw shrimp, shell-on
½ pound medium sea scallops

16 medium mushrooms   *1 green pepper, cut into chunks*
8 cherry tomatoes   *2 medium Bermuda onions*

FOR THE MARINADE:*

½ cup red wine vinegar   *½ teaspoon basil*
½ teaspoon oregano   *1 teaspoon sugar*
¼ teaspoon salt   *Dash of black pepper*
½ cup ketchup   *1 cup oil*

TO PREPARE THE MARINADE:

In a small bowl, mix together all the ingredients except the oil. Add the oil in a slow, steady stream, stirring with a wire whisk until all of it is incorporated. Set aside until needed.

TO PREPARE THE BROCHETTES:

Peel and devein the shrimp.** Using a small sharp knife, remove the

**See Kitchen Notes

skin from the swordfish. Cut the fish into 1½-inch squares, keeping in mind that you want to end up with 16 equal pieces. Quickly rinse the scallops under running water. Drain them and place in a small bowl.

Cut the Bermuda onions into 8 wedges, then set up a work area to assemble the brochettes. Within easy reach you will need 8 skewers, a 9 by 13 by 2 non-metal baking dish, the vegetables, and the seafood.

Begin each skewer with a pepper chunk, (this allows for easy removal), followed by a piece of swordfish, mushroom, a shrimp, onion wedge, then a scallop. Repeat the sequence, ending with a cherry tomato. In this manner, assemble each, laying them in the baking dish as you go.

Re-mix the marinade, then pour it slowly over the length of each brochette so they all benefit from the seasonings. If you run out of marinade before you have covered all the brochettes, simply tip the dish toward one corner and ladle the juices that have collected there.

Cover the dish and refrigerate for 2 hours, going back to it several times to redistribute the marinade as previously described.

Keep in mind that once a marinade has been used for raw fish it must be discarded. Do not attempt to serve it, or save leftovers for another meal.

To cook the brochettes:

These can be cooked under the broiler, but they are really best done on the outside grill. In either case, they should cook about 5 minutes on each side or until the edges of the swordfish are lightly browned. If some areas of your grill are hotter than others, you may need to re-arrange the skewers periodically.

Serve on a bed of rice and enjoy!

---

*If you would rather not make your own marinade, you can use a commercially prepared salad dressing. We particularly like Ken's Caesar Salad and Zesty Italian dressings.

Grilled Yellowfin Tuna
with Tomato Mint Sauce

FOR EACH PERSON, ALLOW:
Allow ½ pound of fresh tuna

FOR THE SAUCE:

1 shallot, diced fine   *½ clove garlic, minced fine*
¼ cup Rose's lime juice   *2 tablespoons fresh mint, chopped*
2 tablespoons olive oil   *2 cups crushed tomatoes*
Salt and pepper to taste

Make the sauce at least 2 hours ahead to let the flavors mingle. Mix all the ingredients together in a small bowl and refrigerate.

You may wish to remove the skin before cooking. This can easily be done by grasping an edge of the skin firmly in one hand and running a small sharp knife between it and the flesh. Quickly rinse under running water to get rid of any scales on the meat. At this point you can either cook your tuna steak in one piece, or divide it into portions.

See the table at left for cooking times and temperatures.

The cold sauce may be served on top, or in a separate side dish.

Inch-thick tuna steaks
on a hot grill:

RARE: *red, cool center*
1 minute/side

MED. RARE: *red, warm*
2 minutes/side

MEDIUM: *pink, firm*
3 minutes/side

MED. WELL: *slightly pink*
4 minutes/side

WELL: *hot, cooked*
5 minutes/side

Grilled Fresh Tuna
with Rosemary Lime Marinade

FOR EACH PERSON, ALLOW:
> *Allow ½ pound of fresh tuna*

FOR THE MARINADE:
> *2 teaspoons fresh rosemary, stems removed, chopped fine*
> *2 teaspoons garlic, diced fine*
> *½ cup of Rose's lime juice*
> *1 cup olive oil*
> *¼ teaspoon white pepper*
> *½ teaspoon salt*

In a small bowl, mix all the ingredients, except the oil. Slowly add the oil in a steady stream, whisking continuously, until it is blended well.

Prepare the tuna by removing the skin as described in the previous recipe. Rinse quickly, pat dry, and cut to portion size. Place the pieces in a glass bowl and pour the marinade over them, turning the fish so that all sides can be exposed to the marinade. Cover and refrigerate for at least 2 hours, turning occasionally to redistribute juices.

When you are ready to cook, take the fish out of the marinade and let it drain for a minute to prevent flare-ups from excess oil. Keep in mind that once a marinade has been used for raw fish it must be discarded. Do not attempt to serve it or to save it for another meal.

See the table at left for cooking times and temperatures.

Grilled Striped Bass
with Fresh Fruit Salsa

FRESH FRUIT SALSAS are a wonderful concept. They make a flavorful, low cholesterol alternative to rich sauces, and they taste great!

This salsa can be made with fruits as they are available. Plums, peaches, nectarines and pears are all appropriate and may be used alone or in combinations. If you choose purple plums, you may want to add yellow peppers as a color contrast. This is a very colorful dish, giving the cook a chance to be creative and dazzle the family or guests!

FOR EACH PERSON, ALLOW:
Allow ½ pound of bass

FOR 2½ CUPS OF FRUIT SALSA:

2 cups of diced fruit	*1 tablespoon lime juice*
2 tablespoons fresh cilantro	*Drizzle of olive oil*
1 tablespoon Bermuda onion	*1 tablespoon tequila*
3 fresh jalapeño peppers,	*Salt to taste*
seeded & diced fine	

Toss all the salsa ingredients together in a glass bowl. The salsa may be served immediately or refrigerated to allow the flavors to blend.

Brush both sides of the fish lightly with oil to keep them from sticking to the grill. Cook for 5 minutes per side, then test with a fork. If fish flakes easily at the thickest part, it is done. If not, continue cooking for 2 minutes on each side; check again for doneness.

Serve the fruit salsa cold on top of grilled bass.

Mako Shark Steak au Poivre

FOR 4 SERVINGS, ALLOW:
> *2 pounds of mako steaks ½- to ¾-inch thick*
> *3 ounces butter or oil*
> *Fresh ground black pepper for dredging the fish*

FOR THE SAUCE:
> *1 clove of garlic, diced fine*
> *4 scallions, cut in ¼-inch slices*
> *½ teaspoon salt*
> *¾ cup dry white wine*

Preheat the oven to 400° F.

Cover both sides of the shark steak with freshly ground pepper. You may want a light sprinkle, or you can coat both sides completely. In a 10-inch skillet, melt the butter. Lay the fish into the pan, cover, and cook on medium heat for 4 minutes on each side.

Transfer the steak to a baking dish and finish cooking in the preheated oven, about 10 minutes.

Meanwhile, use the same 10-inch skillet to make the sauce. Pour the wine into the hot pan, reduce the heat, and cook. Shake the skillet and scrape the sides to loosen the flavorful bits that have remained from the steak and its coating.

Add the salt and garlic, then cook briefly.

A rich, dark brown color, the sauce should be poured onto the fish and served almost immediately after the scallions are added. This will ensure that the scallions keep their vibrant color and that the butter doesn't separate from the sauce to give it an oily appearance and taste.

Bluefish Packets

SOME FAMILIES FIND THEMSELVES with a surplus of bluefish in the summer. before long, they are sharing with friends, neighbors, the mailman, the babysitter, and . . . You get the picture. Here's a simple preparation to help you cope with the seasonal abundance.

FOR EACH PACKET:

½ pound bluefish
1 tablespoon fresh chopped basil   *Fresh ground black pepper*
1 tablespoon minced shallot   *1 tablespoon Marsala*
1 tablespoon thinly-sliced   *Sprinkle of salt*
sundried tomatoes*

* If your sundried tomatoes are not packed in oil, soak them in hot water for a half hour, then drain them before using.

Cut foil in 12-inch squares, one per portion.

Place a piece of fish on each and lay the ingredients on top: first the vegetables, then the Marsala, and finally the seasonings. Fold the foil to make a loose packet around the fish.

TO COOK IN THE OVEN:

Preheat oven to 400° F. Put packets on a sheet pan, place in the oven, and bake for 20 minutes.

TO COOK ON THE GRILL:

Place packets directly over hot flame and cook for 15 minutes.

Grilled Mahi-Mahi
with Black Bean Salsa

Serves 4 to 6

GRILLED FISH, BEANS AND RICE make an easy, well-balanced meal. The Caribbean flavors are a bonus! Try it with a side of bananas or plantains.

FOR EACH PERSON, ALLOW:
> *½ pound of Mahi-Mahi*

FOR THE SALSA:

1 can black beans	*3 tablespoons fresh lime juice*
1 cup cooked corn	*1 teaspoon Worcestershire sauce*
½ small onion, finely diced	*1 tablespoon red wine vinegar*
¼ cup chopped cilantro	*½ teaspoon salt*
1 diced ripe tomato	*½ teaspoon sugar*
1 tablespoon capers	*Fresh ground black pepper*

Combine salsa ingredients and allow to sit for at least an hour.

Brush the fish with a little oil, sprinkle with salt and pepper. Grill it for 4 minutes on each side.

Transfer to individual plates.

Serve with cooked rice and a generous spoonful of salsa.

Garnish with lime.

Grilled Grouper
en Brochette

Serves 4

PLEASING TO THE EYE, as well as to the palate, this heart healthy selection could become a favorite in the hot summer months.

2 pounds grouper fillet
2 Bermuda onions, in wedges
6 cups sliced Romaine lettuce

2 tablespoons fresh tarragon
Lime for garnish

FOR THE LIME TARRAGON MARINADE:

Zest and juice of 1 lime
½ cup Rose's lime juice
¼ cup tarragon vinegar
¼ teaspoon salt

¼ teaspoon white pepper
2 teaspoons sugar
1 cup olive oil

TO PREPARE THE MARINADE:

Blend together all ingredients except the oil. Add the oil in a slow steady stream whisking as you do. Continue whisking until oil is emulsified. Set aside ½ cup marinade to dress the greens.

TO PREPARE THE GROUPER:

Check the fish for bones by laying the fillet on cutting board and running your finger along the center of the fish. Remove any bones with pliers. Cut the fish into 1-inch chunks and drop them into a dish with the marinade. Let stand for 1 hour, stirring once or twice.

Thread the fish onto four skewers, alternating each piece with an onion wedge. Drizzle a little of the marinade over the onions and drain before cooking. Cook on a hot grill, turning once, 5 minutes each side.

While the fish is cooking, set up the plates with a bed of lettuce. When the fish is ready, lay a brochette across each plate, scatter the fresh tarragon on top, and dress the greens with the reserved marinade.

Garnish with lime wedges.

Grilled Salmon Noisettes
with Orange Mint Salsa

Serves 4

WHEN THERE IS AN ABUNDANCE of fresh herbs this easy recipe is a natural! By making the salmon into noisettes, you eliminate skin and bone to make a tidy and attractive little package.

You will need four 6-inch skewers for this operation. If you will be using bamboo skewers, soak them in water for at least an hour so they won't burn on the grill.

> *4 salmon steaks**
> *8 pieces bacon, with as little fat as possible*

> **For best results, select steaks that have a fairly long nape. In other words, select pieces from the center of the salmon rather than from the end.*

FOR THE SALSA:

> *¼ cup finely diced onion*   *½ cup fresh orange juice*
> *¾ cup olive oil*   *6 tablespoons fresh lemon juice*
> *3 tablespoons orange zest*   *½ teaspoon salt*
> *½ cup chopped fresh mint or mint & basil*

Mix salsa ingredients together in a bowl and refrigerate until needed.

TO PREPARE THE SALMON:

Lay the salmon steak on a cutting board and using a very sharp knife, cut between the flesh and the bone. It is easiest to begin at the center of the fish, following the backbone up to the top of the fillet. Do this on both sides of the backbone, then separate the flesh from the rib bones on both sides.

At this point, you should be able to lay the fish out, skin side down and run a knife between the skin and the flesh. Begin in the middle and work out towards the nape, keeping you knife almost parallel to the board. Repeat on the second half.

Run your finger along the fish to feel for any remaining bone. Salmon does have "pin" bones. If you feel any, you will need to remove them with tweezers or small pliers.

That hard part is behind you; it's all glory now!

To prepare the noisettes:

Beginning at the thickest end of the piece, with the skin side out, roll the salmon into a circle, wrap with bacon, and secure with a skewer.

To cook:

Brush the fish on both sides with olive oil, sprinkle with salt and pepper, and cook on a hot grill for 5 minutes per side.

If the outside is browning before the inside is cooked, turn down the heat or move to a cooler part of the grill and cover to finish cooking. Check for doneness by inserting a small sharp knife into the fish. If it is light pink throughout, it is ready.

Serve over wild rice with the salsa drizzled across the fish.

Garnish with mint sprigs and orange rings, cut through the skin to the center and twisted to curl on the plate.

Salmon
Baked in Parchment

Serves 4

BAKED IN THE OVEN or foil wrapped and cooked of the grill, the first steam to escape the packet is so exotic you'll want to bottle it!

2 pounds salmon fillet, skinned and cut into 4 portions

1 lime, cut into 8 thin slices   *Salt & pepper, to taste*
2 tablespoons fresh chopped cilantro   *4 tablespoons sherry*
*1 tablespoon green peppercorns**   *Parchment paper or foil.*

* Green peppercorns are packed in brine and are available at specialty food shops.

Cut four pieces foil or parchment into 12-inch squares. Place a piece of fish on each and top with lime slices, cilantro, and peppercorns. Pour a tablespoon of sherry over the whole and sprinkle with salt and pepper.

Close the foil packets by crimping the edges together. If using parchment, the edges must be alternately folded over and twisted to make them stay together.

To cook the foil packs:

Place on a hot grill and cook for 20 minutes. Move to a cooler spot and continue cooking for 5 to 10 minutes.

To bake in parchment paper:

Preheat oven to 400° F. Put parchment packets on a sheet pan in the oven and cook for 25 minutes.

113

Lobsters
Grilled or Broiled

Q UITE POSSIBLY THE ORIGINAL METHOD of cooking lobsters. Honoring "First People"; yet another reason to cook outdoors in the summer!

If you are squeamish, you'll need to get someone else to prepare the lobsters for you. If there are no volunteers at home, you can ask your fishmonger to do the dirty work.

FOR EACH PERSON:
> *1 lobster, split and cleaned**
> *Melted drawn butter**
> *Lemon wedges for garnish.*

TO GRILL LOBSTERS:

Prepare the fire. When it is reduced to hot coals (medium high on a gas grill) lay the losters over the fire, back side up, for 5 minutes. This will toast the shell a little for flavor. Turn the lobsters onto their back for the remainder of time. Brush with a little butter as soon as you turn them over. The lobster tails will curl as they cook so put a weight on the end of the tail or insert a skewer through the length of the lobster to keep it straight. Cooking times are similar to those for steaming lobsters.*

TO BROIL THE LOBSTERS:

Preheat oven. Lay the lobsters on a broiling pan, back side down, and run a skewer through the length of the tail. If you want, you can mix

*See Kitchen Notes

either lemon juice or tarragon into the drawn butter before you brush the butter on the lobster tail, then cook about 6 inches away from the broiler.

If lobsters are browning too quickly: lower the rack, add a cup of water to the pan, cover loosely with foil, and continue cooking.

Cooking times are similar to those for steaming lobsters.*

New England Clambake

THERE ARE MANY WAYS to construct the clambake; the most traditional is an all day affair. A tarp or canvas large enough to cover the fire and the food is soaked in a barrel of water for several hours. Meanwhile, a pit must be dug early for the fire, then rocks the size of cabbages are used to line the pit. Wood and logs are piled atop the rocks, then the fire is started and burned for a few hours until the rocks are thoroughly heated. When the rocks are the right temperature, the embers are raked away, and the rocks are covered with mounds of wet seaweed. Immediately upon touching the hot rocks, the seaweed begins to steam. Into the steaming weed goes all the food in the reverse order of which it will be served: potatoes, sausage, corn on the cob, lobsters, steamers and mussels. The entire steaming pit is then covered with the soaked tarp and sealed around the edges with sand or cold rocks. Of course, a few beers might be consumed all the while the pit works its magic, and some fresh chowder can satisfy the guests until the time has come. At the proper moment, the bakemaster pulls back the tarp, and volunteers with tongs extract the steaming food, pile it on platters, and serve it to guests.

If you're having trouble imagining yourself pulling the whole thing together, we offer a set of instructions which enable even the rank amateur to prepare a fabulous clambake. Timing is of the essence here, so be organized and follow the timing chart if you must. And don't drink that first beer until the food is actually on the plates.

Kitchen Clambake

Serves 6

YOU'LL NEED NUT-CRACKERS, picks, little dishes for melted butter, cups for clam broth and plenty of napkins. Enjoy and let someone else do the clean-up!

> *6 lobsters, 1¼ pounds each*
> *6 pounds steamers*
> *4 pounds mussels*
> *6 ears of corn*
> *6 Idaho potatoes*
> *6 links Italian sausage*
> *2 lemons*
> *1 pound drawn butter**

If the steamers seem sandy, soak them for 1 hour in cold water to which ½ cup cornmeal has been added. Agitate with your hand once or twice. At the end of the soaking, scoop the clams out of the water and let them drain in a colander. Refrigerate until needed. Discard the soaking liquid.

Inspect and clean the mussels,* then refrigerate until needed.

Scrub the potatoes.

Husk the corn and put it into an appropriate-sized pot or frying pan. Add 2 cups of water, cover, and set on the stove until time to cook.

Follow the cooking schedule on the next pages, counting down to the dinner hour.

*See Kitchen Notes

T MINUS 1 HOUR:

Pierce the potatoes and place them in a preheated 400° F oven.

T MINUS 30 MINUTES:

Put 3 inches of water into the lobster pot and turn it on high

Put the sausages into the oven.

T MINUS 25 MINUTES:

Put the lobsters into the boiling water.

Set up one pot for steamers and one for mussels (or cook them together). Each should have 1½ inches of water. Turn them each on high.

T MINUS 15 MINUTES:

Turn the heat on high under the corn.

Put the steamers and mussels into the boiling water.

T MINUS 10 MINUTES:

Melt the butter on low heat in the microwave; cut lemons.

T MINUS ZERO MINUTES OR THE DINNER HOUR:

Scoop a serving of mussels and steamers onto each plate; top with a lobster and an ear of corn. Serve the baked potato and sausage on a smaller side plate.

Pour steamer broth into individual cups to use for rinsing any sand off the steamers.

You'll need a couple of large bowls on the table to collect all the shells being discarded during the meal.

* *See* Kitchen Notes.

The Autumn Catch

AUTUMN IS OUR FAVORITE SEASON. While spring may bring renewal; summer, the beach; and winter, peace and quiet; fall remains the sweetest season of them all.

Picture this. The days are warm, and the nights are cool. The ocean is even warmer than the air, and that air is crystal clear without a trace of haze or humidity. The summer crush is over, and the locals have money in the bank. Traffic declines by 75 per cent, and fishing is unbelievable.

Is there any nicer season than autumn on Cape Cod, Nantucket & Martha's Vineyard? Is there any more beautiful place to be in September, October, and November? Anywhere in New England? In the world?

Though our own Swan River hardly shows up on most maps of Cape Cod, when it does appear on nautical charts of Nantucket Sound, it might also be called Swan Pond River, because of the shallow pond that serves as its headwaters. As with all the rivers and creeks along this coast, this is not a tributary emptying into the sound, but an estuary, whose currents and depths always ebb and flow, as well as rise and fall with the tides.

As the gull flies, the distance from Swan Pond to Nantucket Sound is only 3 miles or so; however, all of Swan River's meanderings beneath the bridges, through the tidal wetlands, and beside the backyard docks cause its actual length to be even two or three times longer. Because of that, Swan River has long been home to an encyclopedia of sea life.

Fall remains the sweetest season of them all.

119

I remember making coffee some years ago for a team of divers directed by our Natural Resources Department in the Town of Dennis. They surveyed the oyster population in Swan River from our fish market Lower County Road north to the next bridge at Route 28, maybe a two-mile stretch. When they were done, they reached the conclusion that the river was home to some 60,000 bushels of oysters, ranging in size from spat and immature oysters up to those of harvest-size. They also found an abundance of other shellfish, including quahogs, steamers, whelks, crabs, and periwinkles, as well as wide range of finfish.

Just last fall I was mesmerized by an everyday sight which made work difficult. Each time I looked out the window, I could see striped bass jumping right out of the water. Not just one or two, mind you, but dozens and dozen up and down the river. After two or three days, I just couldn't resist the call, so out came the kayak. For the next few days, I was only available by long distance call; that is, people had to shout out from the banks of the river, and I would try to answer their questions. All I did was drift with the current and flow between leaping bass, though I would occasionally hook one up just for the fun of it.

As you might expect, I couldn't help but reflect on all those poor people whose work kept them cooped-up in offices and cities. Unfortunately, they had no idea that on days like those you wish for time to stand still and for life to last forever. Clearly, there is no nicer season than autumn on our peninsula and islands.

And, oh yes, the fish.

The Atlantic reaches its warmest temperature in August. And though September brings cooler weather, the aquatic life is at its zenith. Giant bluefin tuna abound off Chatham and on up Stellwagen Bank. The biggest bluefish and striped bass of the season are fattening-up for their migration south. Though not for long, swordfish are still in our waters, and even lobsters are more abundant. The fall run can often be the most productive period of the season, and this is truly a time to be thankful, well before Thanksgiving. Change is definitely in the air.

Fall brings to our fish market two of the most anticipated seasonal

The fall run can often be the most productive period of the season, and this is truly a time to be thankful, well before Thanksgiving.

delicacies: Wellfleet oysters and Cape bay scallops. Both have been the subjects of books on their own, and both deserve them.

Wives' tales of old have it that oysters should only be eaten during months with an R in them. That season runs from September to April. While that tale is not true, oysters in the fall and winter do have a decidedly better consistency and flavor. They spawn in the warmer months, so they often are found to be watery and clear. As the water cools, however, oysters become much more appealing, firm and white. Of course, if you must have an oyster in July or August, those coldwater Wellfleets, as well as those from Cotuit, will still satisfy.

At Swan River we have had the same folks from Wellfleet bringing them to us for more than twenty-five years. Woody and Peggy are as knowledgeable about oysters as any people I know. They have made oysters their life. They harvest both wild and farmed oysters from their own grant, and they have seen entire crops of oysters destroyed by mysterious aquatic diseases. They've suffered storm damage from hurricanes and nor'easters, but they keep on oystering. If Wellfleet has any oysters to harvest at all, Woody and Peggy arrive at the market, smiling away.

Howard Snow was another Wellfleet original from whom I had the pleasure to buy. What a character! Back in the '70s, when he was in his own seventies, Howard would show up at our back door. With a red bandana holding back his long, grey hair and his watery blue eyes twinkling, he'd ask how we were set for oysters. I'd tell him to bring in four bushels, and I'd ask him what took him so long to get here from Wellfleet. He'd toss his head in the direction of the front seat of his truck. There sat a winsome, free-spirited, young girl, twenty-something, and Howard would say, "Well, I picked her up hitchhiking on the way here, and we decided to go skinny-dipping." True story. Howard passed away a few years ago on a cold winter day. Howard was found on the beach in Wellfleet, no more fitting place for him to go.

There are many ways to eat oysters, all satisfying. But the absolute finest is simply the way nature prepares them. Raw and *au natural*. I've even tested them from a digger with my morning coffee. Their flavor is

Wives' tales of old say that oysters should only be eaten during those months that have an R in them. While that tale is not true, oysters in the fall and winter do have a decidedly better consistency and flavor.

so delicate and unique that no condiment in the world could ever do them justice.

The true art to opening oysters is also lost on too many people. A properly-shucked oyster should be opened carefully enough so that the oysters meat remains intact, not cut. The opened oyster also should never be rinsed with freshwater. The liquor within the oyster holds much of the flavor and saltiness.

Cape bay scallops are the second seafood treat to arrive in the fall. The season opens on different days throughout the Cape & Islands, but it creates as much anticipation and excitement around here as deer-hunting season does elsewhere. Everyone wants to know: Which towns have good harvests? Which got shut out? Where will the action be this year?

The effect of a good scallop season will be felt throughout a town all winter long. Unfortunately, the good years are becoming more rare. Chatham hasn't seen a good year for a dozen years. Dennis had an extraordinary harvest only a few years ago, possibly the best ever. Without a doubt, bay scallop harvests have been declining for years. A wise old fisherman once told me, "You'll never get scallops unless there is eelgrass." Eelgrass is the straight, green seaweed that grows in rivers and bays. It has been disappearing rapdily throughout our region due to development and pollution run-off. It's a Cape Cod curse. Our beauty is our demise.

Meanwhile, we are fortunate to have Nantucket fishermen selling to us all winter long. A great many people do not realize that the island is the richest bay scallop fishery along the entire Eastern seaboard. Only a handful of watermen work through our severe winters. Often, their catch is flown to us by small plane whenever the ferry is unable to make it back to the Cape.

Bay scallops have become a generic term for small scallops from all over the world: Chinese bays, Peruvian bays, Icelandic bays, Mexican bays, and Carolina bays, just to name a few. The average price for these imported bays is $2 to $3 per pound; however, we pay our island fishermen more than $10 per pound all winter long, and that should say all

A great many people do not realize that Nantucket Island is the richest bay scallop fishery along the entire Eastern seaboard.

that must be said about the difference between these products. They may all share a name, but bays from the Cape & Islands are like no others.

Unfortunately, summer visitors to Cape Cod, Nantucket & Martha's Vineyard never get to experience the taste of fresh Cape scallops. There really is no comparison to any other scallop. Certainly, ours must have a high natural sugar content, because they are the sweetest things you'll ever eat that isnt a dessert! Often out on the boat we would eat them right from the shell.

Local bay scallops are wonderful eating in any preparation. We enjoy them deep-fried, in stews, in stir-fries, in Newburgs, or in casseroles. The possibilities are really endless, but the first scallops of the season are always cooked the same simple way in our house. Place them in a glass baking dish, sprinkle with unseasoned bread crumbs, put a few pats of butter on top, and broil for about 5 minutes. Let the great taste of the scallops provide the seasoning. There really is nothing like it.

Harvesting scallops was one of the greatest thrills of my fishing adventures. If the Scallop Gods permit, they are found in bays and rivers close to shore throughout the Cape & Islands. Often we would be fishing in little coves and channels well-protected from rough seas. The process consists of towing two to four 100-pound dredges along the bay bottom until they are full of whatever is down there. We would simply stop the boat, pull the dredges on board, and cull through the contents.

Of course, once you had your limit and you headed for shore, your day was only half over. You still had to shuck your catch, which remains a boring process. Back then, our legal limit was 20 bushels, with each bushel containing hundreds of scallops. I still remember being so tired by the end of the day that we would virtually be rocking back and forth as though we were still on the boat. We'd check with each other: "My boat's rocking. How 'bout yours?" Some nights we would finish shucking our catch at 10:00 or 11:00 at night, only to be rising again at 5:00 the next morning to head out in the boat again.

Fortunately, the various towns usually dont allow commercial scalloping on Sundays, and I have never known any relaxation since like

Unfortunately, summer visitors to the Cape & Islands never get to experience the taste of fresh Cape scallops.

those Sundays during scallop season. The days of a fisherman remain much like that on a year round basis, and I have tremendous respect for their work ethic. For all the bad press that the fishing industry has received because of overfishing, I would love to see one of their armchair critics try to keep up with a fishermans pace for a week.

The other day, I read an interesting article in an industry magazine called *Seafood Leader*. "Fishermen harvest what they're allowed to harvest," wrote Roger Fitzgerald. "Catching as many fish as they can is how they make their living. Regulating them is how [fishery] managers make theirs. If a stock is depleted, it's not because of greedy fishermen: it's because of mismanagement. Period." I think that puts it perfectly. Don't blame fishermen for catching too many fish. Only 20 years ago the government was encouraging fishermen to build bigger and better boats in order to catch more fish.

But I digress.

Let's eat.

Don't blame fishermen for catching too many fish.

An Autumn Menu

Appetizer
Smoked Bluefish Paté
Broiled Oysters on the Half Shell
Oysters Rockefeller
Steamed Oysters: West Coast Style
Stuffed Cherrystone Clams
Cape Scallop Appetizer

Soup
Oyster & Spinach Stew
Smoked Salmon Chowder
Cape Scallop Stew

Entrées
Mussels Steamed with Garlic & Wine
Broiled Cape Scallops
Sole Almondine
Flounder Pinwheels with Mushroom Marsala Sauce
Baked Fish with Pesto
Mussels Palermo
Lobster Pie
Crabmeat Enchiladas
Shrimp Burritos

Grilled Tuna with Wilted Greens & Balsamic Onions
Grouper with Sweet Potato Crust
Jerk Seasoned Halibut with Apple Ginger Chutney
Seafood Creole
Paella
Lobster Sauté

Smoked Bluefish Paté

Yields about 1½ cups

THIS PATÉ IS QUITE VERSATILE. Served with crackers, it can be either molded into a shape on a plate, or put into a crock. Using a star attachment on a pastry bag, you could pipe the paté onto Melba toast or cucumber slices and garnish with fresh dill.

½ pound smoked bluefish
4 ounces cream cheese
1½ teaspoons horseradish
1½ teaspoons lemon juice
1 teaspoon chopped fresh dill
¼ cup light cream

Remove skin and break up the bluefish, checking carefully for bones. Put the fish, plus all the remaining ingredients (except the cream) into a blender or food processor. Stopping at least once to scrape down the sides of the bowl, blend until everything is chopped well.

With the machine still running, add the cream in a steady stream. Process for a minute or two, stopping when the mixture is a smooth paste.

Place in a covered dish and refrigerate until serving.

Broiled Oysters
on the Halfshell

Serves 4

A GREAT PREPARATION for the "first time" oyster eater!

24 oysters   *Bread crumbs*
Dash of Tabasco   *¼ cup melted butter*
Lemon juice

Preheat the broiler.

While shucking the oysters* , save the bottom shells, because they are shaped like shallow bowls and hold the juice quite nicely during cooking. If available, rock salt makes a great bed for cooking oysters. It stabilizes the shells in the oven, holds the heat, and provides an elegant look that can be taken to the table or buffet.

Arrange oysters in their halfshells on a broiling pan. Add to each: a dash of Tabasco, a few drops of lemon juice, a sprinkle of bread crumbs and a teaspoon of melted butter.

Place the tray about 6 inches beneath the broiler and cook briefly until the crumbs are lightly browned and the edges of the oysters begin to curl. Serve hot with narrow wedges of lemon.

*See Kitchen Notes

Oysters Rockefeller

Serves 6

THIS IS THE SWAN RIVER VERSION of a classic oyster appetizer.

3 dozen opened oysters* on the halfshell

4 tablespoons butter	*¾ cup of bread crumbs*
½ cup onion, diced finely	*2 tablespoons Pernod*
1 package frozen spinach	*Salt and pepper to taste*

Defrost the spinach, then chop and squeeze it to remove excess liquid. Sauté the onions in the butter until they are golden brown. Remove them from the heat and add the Pernod. Return to heat and reduce the liquid slightly by cooking for another minute. Put the onions and their juices into a bowl and mix in the spinach, bread crumbs, salt and pepper.

Preheat the oven to 400° F.

Arrange the opened oysters in a shallow baking dish (on a bed of rock salt if it is available.) Place about 2 tablespoons of stuffing mix on each oyster.

(At this point, they may be refrigerated to cook later.)

Bake for about 10 minutes or until the topping browns. Keep in mind that they will take longer to cook if they have been in the refrigerator.

*See Kitchen Notes

Steamed Oysters
West Coast Style

Serves 4

LONG TIME EMPLOYEE, Memi Chin brings us this recipe from one of her many off-season trips to California. Thanks, Memi; we love this tasty treatment for our Cape Cod oysters!

24 oysters	*4 scallions, greens sliced*
3 cloves garlic	*Sesame oil*
3 tablespoons oil	*Soy sauce*
Piece of fresh ginger equivalent in size to the three cloves of garlic	

In a blender or food processor, chop the garlic and ginger until quite fine. Put into a small jar and cover with the oil. This is a handy mix which will keep well in your refrigerator if you don't use it all for the oysters.

Open the oysters* and discard the top shell. Top each oyster with ¼ teaspoon garlic mix, a drop of sesame oil, a drop of soy sauce, and a sprinkling of scallions. Let the oysters marinate for 10 minutes.

Using a steamer in a wok or a shallow water bath in a skillet, steam the oysters for 3 or 4 minutes or until the edges begin to curl.

Serve immediately.

*See Kitchen Notes

Stuffed Cherrystone Clams

Makes 24

A STUFFED CLAM served with a juicy lemon wedge is a fine way to stave off hunger while you wait for dinner to cook.

2 dozen cherrystone clams, rinsed

1 cup diced onion	*2 tablespoons sherry*
½ cup diced red pepper	*1 tablespoon Worcestershire sauce*
½ cup diced green pepper	*½ teaspoon Tabasco*
2 tablespoons minced garlic	*6 cups bread crumbs*
6 tablespoons melted butter	*Reserved broth from clams*
1 teaspoon fennel seed, mashed	*Paprika*

Rinse clams and place in large frying pan or Dutch oven. Add about 1 cup water, cover the pan, and cook at high temperature until all the clams are open (about 10 minutes from the time the water begins to boil). Do not overcook clams, as they will shrink and toughen.

Drain off the broth and reserve for use in stuffing.

Allow the clams to cool, remove the meats from the shell, then chop them or grind in a meat grinder. (Grinding is preferable if you are making multiples of this recipe). Refrigerate clam meat *and* shells until needed.

Put half the uncooked vegetables into a large mixing bowl.

Heat a sauté pan, add 2 tablespoons melted butter, and sauté the remaining vegetables until the onions are clear. Transfer them to the bowl.

Heat together 3 tablespoons melted butter, the fennel seeds, the sherry,

Worcestershire sauce, and Tabasco. Pour into the bowl, then add in the clams and bread crumbs. Mix well and add in some clam broth. The amount of liquid needed will vary according to the type of bread crumbs used *and* personal taste. By adding ¼ cup of broth at a time, you will be able to reach a workable consistency without making a soggy mess. If you take a tablespoon of the stuffing and squeeze it lightly in your hand, it should hold together.

Arrange the clam shells on a baking pan with low sides. Distribute the stuffing mix equally among the shells, then pack and shape each with your hands. A light touch is called for here; no need to make dense little dough balls. Garnish by brushing with melted butter and sprinkling with paprika.

The clams may by heated and served right away, or you might wish to wrap them individually and freeze them to use a few at a time.

To cook DIRECTLY:

Preheat oven to 350° F. Cook for 25 to 30 minutes.

To cook from the freezer:

Microwave for 3 minutes, then put into a (preheated) toaster oven and cook for 5 to 10 minutes until the top is slightly browned.

Cape Scallop Appetizer

WHILE DIJON AND CHUTNEY MIGHT APPEAR to make an unseemly combination, this is a wonderful taste treat!

3 to 4 ounces of bay scallops   *1 tablespoon chutney*
1 tablespoon Dijon mustard   *2 teaspoons butter*

In a sauté pan of appropriate size, melt the butter, then add the scallops and cook on medium heat for 5 minutes. Stir in the mustard and chutney and continue cooking until it is heated through.

Serve on scallop shells with a parsley garnish.

Oyster & Spinach Stew

Serves 4 to 6

OYSTER STEW DOES NOT WANT TO WAIT to be served. Once it is hot, it will curdle easily, and the oysters will quickly overcook.

1 pint fresh shucked oysters* and their juice
1 12-ounce package frozen leaf spinach or 5-ounces of fresh spinach
6 tablespoons butter   2 cups of light cream
6 tablespoons flour   Pinch of white pepper
2 cups of fish stock*   Pinch of nutmeg
3 shallots, diced

Frozen spinach should be thawed, squeezed dry, and chopped; fresh spinach should have stems and tough leaves removed, then be rinsed and steamed until limp before it is chopped.

Melt 4 tablespoons of the butter in a 4-quart saucepan. Add the shallots and cook until they are done, then add the flour. Cook over medium heat, stirring frequently, for about 5 minutes. Slowly stir in the fish stock with a wire whisk until the mixture is smooth. Add the cream in the same manner and continue stirring as it thickens.

Add the spinach and seasonings. Reduce the heat to low and stir periodically while preparing the oysters.

In a medium frying pan, melt 2 tablespoons of butter and add the oysters. Cook on medium heat just until the edges of the oysters begin to curl. Combine cooked oysters and juices with the cream mixture.

Heat well and serve.

*See Kitchen Notes

Smoked Salmon Chowder

Serves 6

AT SWAN RIVER we are fortunate to have a large smoker *and* an accomplished chef to oversee the smoking of a variety of seafoods, including top quality salmon, a key flavor in this chowder.

¾ pound fresh salmon fillet	2½ cups fish stock* total
¼ pound smoked salmon	3 tablespoons flour
5 slices bacon, in ½-inch pieces	2 cups milk or light cream
½ cup chopped onion	½ teaspoon salt
½ cup chopped pepper	¼ teaspoon white pepper
2 cups diced potatoes	½ teaspoon dried dill
10-ounce frozen mixed vegetables	1 tablespoon fresh chopped parsley

In a small pan cook the potatoes until tender. Drain and set aside.

Bring 2 cups of water to a boil, carefully add in the salmon, then reduce the heat and poach gently for 10 to 15 minutes. Lift out the salmon, break it into coarse chunks and set aside to cool. Reserve the cooking liquid and add stock to make 2½ cups total.

Heat a 3- or 4-quart saucepan, then cook the bacon until it is crisp. Remove the bacon pieces, then cook the onion and pepper in the fat.

Add in the flour, and stir briefly until flour is blended in well.

Slowly stir in the stock with a wire whisk to eliminate lumps. Allow the mixture to come to a boil before adding the vegetables and seasonings, then cook together for 10 minutes. Add the fish and cream, then continue cooking gently until everything is heated through.

Salmon is a very delicate fish. Once it has been added to the chowder, stir very carefully to prevent the fish from breaking down completely.

*See Kitchen Notes

Cape Scallop Stew

THIS IS THE WAY most Cape fishermen eat their scallops!

FOR EACH PERSON, ALLOW:
4 to 6 ounces of Cape scallops
1 small pat of butter
1 tablespoon finely chopped shallots
1 cup cream or milk
Salt and pepper to taste

Heat the cream slowly while preparing the scallops.

In a frying pan of appropriate size, melt the butter, add the shallots, and cook on medium heat for a few minutes until the shallots are tender and clear. Add the scallops and cook for about 5 minutes, tossing the pan lightly once or twice to ensure even cooking. Look for the scallops to firm up slightly and give off a milky liquid. At this point, add the hot cream, salt and pepper. Leave the stew on the heat until it is piping hot, remembering that scallops take very little time to cook to perfection.

Spoon the stew into bowls and serve, adding a few finely sliced scallions or a sprinkle of paprika to garnish.

Mussels Steamed
with Garlic & Wine

Serves 8 as an appetizer, 6 as a lunch, or 4 as a dinner

THE MUSSEL LOVER'S FAVORITE! Serve this in large shallow bowls with the broth, along with plenty of crisp French bread for dipping.

6 pounds of mussels, cleaned and de-bearded*

4 cloves of garlic, minced	*½ cup butter*
1 tablespoon chopped parsley	*½ cup water*
½ cup white wine	

In a small saucepan, melt the butter, add the garlic and cook gently for 5 minutes.

Add in the wine, water, and parsley.

Heat the mixture for 5 more minutes, and it is ready to use.

Place the mussels into a large pan, such as a 6-quart Dutch oven. Pour the broth over them and cook on medium to high heat.

Once a good head of steam develops, reduce the heat so the broth doesn't boil over.

Steam the mussels for 5 to 10 minutes until all the shells are opened.

*See Kitchen Notes

Broiled Cape Scallops

Serves 4

EVERY TIME I PLAN TO COOK CAPE SCALLOPS at home, I go over possible recipes and methods of preparation. I keep telling myself that I really should try something new and different; however, 9 times out of 10 this is how I end up preparing them. It's so simple and delicious, I reason, why mess with perfection?

1½ pounds of scallops	*2 scallions (optional)*
¼ cup melted butter	*Salt & pepper, to taste*
½ cup bread crumbs	

Preheat the broiler.

Place the scallops in a shallow baking dish suitable for broiling. They should be packed closely together, but not piled up. Pour a little melted butter over the top and sprinkle with a light coating of bread crumbs. Cook under the broiler, not too close to the heat, for about 10 minutes. (Sometimes I will mix in a few finely-sliced scallions midway through the cooking. This gives me a chance to check their progress and add a little subtle flavor.) The crumbs should be golden brown and the scallop meats should be solid white throughout.

Cape scallops are so tender that it is easy to be fooled as to whether or not they are cooked. Don't worry about undercooking them, though, because scallops can be eaten raw!

Sole Almondine

Serves 4

IN THE SEAFOOD WORLD, there is nothing as delicate as the taste of fresh sole. Add to it the sweet, nutty flavor of buttered almonds, and you have a combination that is sure to please the most discriminating palate!

2 pounds of fresh sole fillet

½ cup sliced almonds   *1 tablespoon lemon juice*
¼ cup butter or margarine   *Pinch of salt*

Begin by melting the butter with the salt and lemon juice. Put the almonds into a bowl and pour the butter mix over them, stirring to coat the almonds.

Preheat the oven to 400° F.

Using melted butter or margarine, brush the bottom of a shallow baking dish and lay the fillets, skin side down into it. (The fillet will not actually have the skin on it, but we put this side down for cosmetic reasons. The skin side can be determined by silvery traces and slightly darker coloration.) Top each piece with almonds and bake for 10 minutes, or until the almonds are golden brown, and the fish flakes easily with a fork.

Using a long metal spatula, carefully transfer the fish to warm dinner plates and serve.

Flounder Pinwheels
with Mushroom Marsala Sauce

Serves 4

THIS SWAN RIVER ORIGINAL LOOKS GREAT, and it tastes even better. Use it when you want to show off. The dish can be prepared up to one day in advance; just pop it in the oven when you're ready.

2 pounds medium flounder fillets, somewhat uniform in size.

FOR THE PINWHEELS:

1 package of frozen spinach, chopped
¼ cup sweet red pepper, diced fine
6 to 8 ounces Swiss cheese, sliced thin
2 shallots, diced fine

FOR THE SAUCE:

1 cup sliced mushrooms	*4 tablespoons flour*
3 tablespoons butter or margarine	*¼ cup Marsala*
1½ cups fish stock*, heated	*Salt & pepper, to taste*

TO PREPARE THE SAUCE:

Melt the butter in a medium sauté pan, add the mushrooms and cook for 5 minutes, tossing the pan lightly to ensure even cooking. Add the flour, then continue cooking and stirring for 2 to 3 minutes. Combine the fish stock and Marsala, then slowly pour it into the mushroom/flour mix, stirring with a wire whisk to prevent lumps from forming. Add salt and pepper to taste, then simmer for 5 to 10 minutes, stirring periodically, until thickened. Set aside.

*See Kitchen Notes

TO PREPARE THE PINWHEELS:

Mix together in a bowl the spinach, the red peppers, and the shallots. Lay a piece of fish upon a clean work surface, skin side up. Cover the fillet with a slice of cheese, then a thin layer of the spinach mix.

Beginning with the thin end of the fillet, roll the fish. Holding both sides firmly, cut down through the center of the roll with a very sharp knife. Place these two sections, cut-side up, in a shallow baking dish. It takes a little manipulating to keep the pinwheels upright and tightly-rolled and you may wish to use toothpicks to keep them in line. Just be sure to remove them after baking.

At this point you could cover and refrigerate the fish and sauce separately, or you could proceed to the next phase of preparation.

TO PREPARE THE MEAL:

Heat the sauce while the fish is cooking.

Preheat the oven to 400° F.

Put ½ cup of water in the pan with the fish, cover tightly with foil, and bake for 10 to 15 minutes. If you are using a glass dish, or if the preparation has been kept in the refrigerator for any period of time, you may need to cook a little longer. In any case, check for doneness by taking a peek inside one of the rolls. The cheese should be melted, and the fish should flake easily with a fork.

TO PRESENT THE MEAL:

When the fish comes out of the oven you may wish to strain the juices from the baking dish into the sauce. It is not completely necessary, but it will add to the flavor. Rest a mesh strainer over the sauce pot. Holding the fish back with a spatula, gently tip the baking dish so that the juices can run out of one corner, through the strainer and into the sauce. Blend in the juices, then ladle about ¼-inch layer of sauce onto a heated platter or individual dinner plates. Place the pinwheels on the sauce and serve.

Extra sauce can be served in a separate dish.

Baked Fish with Pesto

FREQUENTLY IN THE EARLY FALL, we are inundated with fresh basil. What better use is there for basil than to make pesto? And what better use is there for pesto than spread upon a fresh piece of fish for baking?

Many types of fish qualify for this special treatment. We have used tilefish with wonderful results, as well as whitefish, ocean catfish, and monkfish. Even shellfish, such as shrimp and scallops, succumb to the charms of pesto. Select the best from the fish counter and you will be on your way to a fine meal.

FOR EACH PERSON, ALLOW:
½ pound of fish

FOR THE PESTO:

1 cup of fresh basil	*½ cup olive oil*
2 cloves of garlic, diced	*¾ cup Parmesan cheese*
½ cup pine nuts	*Dash of fresh black pepper*

This recipe yields a very flavorful mixture so a thin layer on top of the fish is all you will need. If there is any left over, it can be kept in the refrigerator or freezer for another use.

Remove the coarse stems of the basil, as well as any shriveled leaves, rinse, then pack into the cup for measurement.

Place all the ingredients into a blender or food processor, then blend until it forms a smooth paste, stopping once or twice to scrape down the sides of the bowl.

Preheat the oven to 400° F.

Put the fish into a shallow baking dish, spread the pesto on top and bake, allowing 10 minutes per inch measured through the thickest part of the fish. Test with a fork or sharp knife for doneness. The fish should be opaque throughout and flake easily.

Mussels Palermo

Makes a first course for 6, or a hearty entrée for 4

ONCE YOU GET PAST THE CHOPPING of vegetables and cleaning of mussels, this tasty concoction can be put together quickly. If you are short of time at the dinner hour, you can do the prep earlier in the day, put the ingredients into little bowls on a tray in the refrigerator, then toss it altogether like a pro at the appointed hour.

6 pounds mussels in the shell*
4 tablespoon olive oil
20 whole black olives
4 cloves of garlic, diced
1 cup cherry tomatoes, quartered
12 pepperoncini, in ½-inch sections, stems removed

1 cup mushrooms, quartered
1 cup leeks, in ½-inch slices
½ cup Marsala
½ teaspoon salt
Fresh ground black pepper

Linguine for 4 people (only when used as an entrée)

Steam the mussels and remove them from the shells.*

While you are preparing everything else, cook the linguine according to package directions. Cook it *al dente*, because it will be heated again and could easily overcook.

In a 10-inch to 12-inch skillet heat the oil, add the garlic, and cook briefly. Next add the leeks and mushrooms, tossing the pan a few times to coat everything with oil. Cook over medium heat for 5 minutes, stirring frequently. Once the white ends of the leeks are clear, add the cherry

*See Kitchen Notes

tomatoes, pepperoncini, olives, seasonings and Marsala. Cover and simmer gently for 5 minutes, then test a leek to be sure it is tender throughout.

Once the leeks are cooked, add in the cooked mussel meats and hot linguine. Cook another 5 minutes until it is piping hot.

Two notes of caution may be needed. First, this dish is best when the vegetables are just cooked, because overcooking causes them to loose their shape and color. Second, once the mussels have been added, either stir carefully, or shake the pan so that you don't break up the mussel meats.

Using a spaghetti lifter, take out the pasta first, then ladle the rest over top.

Have Parmesan cheese and a peppermill available on the table.

Lobster Pie

Serves 4 to 6

A WONDERFUL TREAT for a special occasion dinner!

1 to 1½ pounds of lobster meat

FOR THE BISCUIT CRUST:

2 cups of flour	*3 tablespoons butter*
4 teaspoon of baking powder	*1 teaspoon tarragon*
½ teaspoon of salt	*1 cup milk or light cream*
1 tablespoon sugar	

FOR THE SAUCE:

4 tablespoons flour	*1 tablespoon sherry*
4 tablespoons butter or margarine	*½ cup grated cheddar cheese*
*1 cup fish stock**	*½ teaspoon tarragon*
1 cup whole milk or light cream	*1 teaspoon Dijon mustard*
1 tablespoon shallots, finely diced	*Pinch of white pepper*

TO PREPARE THE BISCUITS:

Mix the dry ingredients. Cut in the butter until the mixture resembles coarse corn meal, then stir in the milk. Mix only until blended together, then turn the dough onto a floured board or countertop. Roll the dough to a ¾-inch thickness and cut into round shapes, 4 inches in diameter.

TO PREPARE THE SAUCE:

Melt the butter in a small saucepan. Add the shallots and cook, stir-

*See Kitchen Notes

ring for 4 or 5 minutes. Add the flour, stir, and cook for about 5 more minutes on medium heat. Blend the sherry into the stock, then pour this mixture slowly into the pan, stirring constantly with a wire whisk. When the stock is hot and blended, add the remaining items. Reduce heat and cook, stirring frequently, until sauce is hot and thickened. Add salt to taste, remembering that commercial bouillon has quite a bit of salt. Set the sauce aside while you prepare the lobster meat.

To prepare the pie:

Preheat the oven to 375° F.

Remove any cartilage and veins from the lobster meat, then cut into bite-sized pieces. Place the meat into a shallow baking dish and cover with sauce. Arrange the crusts on top. Bake for 20 minutes or until the biscuit topping is golden brown, and the edges of the sauce are bubbling.

Crabmeat Enchiladas

Serves 4

WARM UP A COOL AUTUMN NIGHT with this spicy entrée from south of the border. Serve with Spanish rice and refried beans to complete the feast.

> 1 pound crabmeat
> 1 medium onion, diced
> 2 cups shredded cheddar cheese
>
> 2 10-ounce cans enchilada sauce
> 12 corn tortillas

Combine the crabmeat, onions, and cheese to make the filling.

Each enchilada portion will consist of the tortillas stacked in three layers, so you will need a 9-by-12 baking dish to hold a layer of four tortillas.

Spread a thin covering of enchilada sauce on the bottom of the baking dish.

Heat a heavy bottom fry pan over medium heat. Warm each tortilla just until it is flexible and place the first four in the bottom layer of sauce to begin the stacks. Top each with crabmeat filling, another warmed tortilla, and repeat the layering. Pour over the remaining sauce over the enchiladas, wrap loosely with foil, and heat in the oven for 20 minutes at 400° F.

Garnish with sour cream and chopped scallions.

Shrimp Burritos

Makes 6-8

THIS IS GREAT FAMILY FARE as each person may assemble his or her own, omitting or adding ingredients according to taste.

1 pound raw shrimp, peeled and deveined*

2 tablespoons oil	*¼ cup sliced black olives*
1 pack low-salt taco seasoning	*Tomato salsa, to taste*
2 cups shredded iceberg lettuce	*Sour cream*
½ cup diced onion	*Refried black beans (optional)*
1½ cups shredded cheddar cheese	*1½ cups diced tomatoes*

6-8 soft flour tortillas

TO PREPARE THE FILLING:

Coarsely chop the raw shrimp.

Heat a medium saucepan, add 2 tablespoons oil, then the shrimp. Cook for a minute or two, stirring constantly.

Add the taco seasoning and just enough water to make a thick sauce. Cover and simmer gently for 5 minutes adjusting the water if necessary.

TO ASSEMBLE THE BURRITOS:

Arrange the remaining burrito fillings in bowls near the stove for ease of production.

Put a large frying pan on medium heat and grill each tortilla for 1 minute per side.

*See Kitchen Notes

Assemble each by laying fillings across the center of a tortilla and rolling to form a burrito about 1½ inches in diameter.

With so many ingredients it's easy to build an oversize, unmanageable burrito. Think small when you begin, and it will probably come out just right.

Grilled Tuna
with Wilted Greens & Balsamic Onions

Serves 4

IF YOU END UP with more of the caramelized balsamic onion than you need for one meal, fear not! This concoction is great with pork, beef, or lamb. Make it ahead and bring it out when you are ready to eat.

2 pounds fresh tuna steaks

4 to 6 cups kale, rinsed and cut in ½-inch strips
2 cloves garlic, minced
2 tablespoons olive oil
Lemon wedges, for garnish

FOR THE CARAMELIZED BALSAMIC ONIONS:

4 onions, sliced thin   *¾ cup sugar*
1 cup red wine   *¼ teaspoon thyme*
½ cup balsamic vinegar   *¼ teaspoon black pepper*
½ cup red wine vinegar

In a heavy saucepan over high heat, caramelize the onions (without oil or water), stirring frequently until they are wilted and quite dark in color. Add in the remaining ingredients, then cook on low heat until the mixture is thick, like marmalade.

The whole process may take an hour or more, so stir often and check heat to be sure sugar from the onions is not burning on the bottom of the pan.

Remove from heat, allow to cool.

TO COOK THE TUNA:

Brush both sides of the fish with oil, season with salt and pepper. Cook on a hot grill, timed according to your preference.

TO COOK THE GREENS:

While the tuna is cooking, heat a wok or large frying pan. Add in the oil, then the kale. Cook quickly, stirring or tossing with tongs to cook evenly.

When it as almost wilted, add the garlic and season with salt and pepper.

Remove from heat while it is still bright green; better to let it cool a little than let it turn khaki brown while you wait for the tuna to cook.

When the tuna is cooked, transfer the kale to individual plates and arrange in circles about 6 inches in diameter. Place a piece of tuna in the center of each serving.

Top with a generous tablespoon of the caramelized balsamic onion and garnish with lemon wedges.

Inch-thick tuna steaks on a hot grill:

RARE: *red, cool center*
1 minute/side

MED. RARE: *red, warm*
2 minutes/side

MEDIUM: *pink, firm*
3 minutes/side

MED. WELL: *slightly pink*
4 minutes/side

WELL: *hot, cooked*
5 minutes/side

Grouper
with Sweet Potato Crust

Serves 4

THIS PREPARATION WORKS WELL with any of the firm fish; tuna, swordfish, halibut, striped bass, or mahi-mahi.

2 pounds fish (no thicker than ¾ inch)

1 large sweet potato   *¼ teaspoon nutmeg*
½ teaspoon salt   *Dijon mustard*
½ teaspoon white pepper

Preheat oven to 400° F.

Peel the potato and grate it into a bowl.

Mix in the salt, pepper, ginger and nutmeg.

Place the fish in a lightly oiled, shallow baking dish. Spread a little mustard onto each piece, then top with a thin layer of shredded sweet potato.

Bake for 20 minutes, then check for doneness.*

Serve as soon as the fish is cooked through.

*See Kitchen Notes

Jerk Seasoned Halibut
with Apple Ginger Chutney

Serves 4

JAMAICAN JERK SEASONINGS give a spicy, smoky flavor to the mild halibut. Serve over wild rice with apple ginger chutney for an exciting combination of tastes.

> *2 pounds fresh halibut*
> *Jerk seasoning powder*

FOR THE APPLE GINGER CHUTNEY:

> *4 tart apples, sliced, not peeled*
> *¼ cup raisins*
> *1 tablespoon fresh ginger, sliced thin*
> *¼ cup balsamic vinegar*
> *¼ cup sugar*

TO MAKE THE CHUTNEY:

Put ingredients into a small heavy saucepan. Simmer on low heat for about 30 minutes, stirring frequently until fruit is reduced to a jam-like consistency.

TO PREPARE THE HALIBUT:

Coat both sides of the halibut with jerk seasoning and cook under the broiler or on the grill.

Serve on a bed of wild rice, garnish with chutney, fresh lime and apple slices.

Seafood Creole

Serves 6 to 8

THIS LONG STANDING FAVORITE at Swan River Restaurant can be made in stages and cooked at the last minute for guests or family. Serve over rice for a very hearty meal.

1½ pounds firm white fish (haddock, halibut, grouper, or monkfish)

12 littleneck clams, in the shell   *½ pound uncooked shrimp*
12 mussels, in the shell   *6 ounces cooked lobster meat*
½ pound scallops

FOR THE CREOLE SAUCE:

3 tablespoons olive oil   *¼ lemon*
4 ounces ham, diced   *1 teaspoon Tabasco*
½ cup diced onions   *1 tablespoon Worcestershire sauce*
½ cup diced peppers   *¼ teaspoon thyme*
1 tablespoon minced garlic *¼ teaspoon fresh ground black pepper*
½ cup diced celery   *¼ teaspoon white pepper*
10-ounce frozen okra   *½ cup red wine*
32-ounce can crushed tomatoes

TO PROCESS THE SEAFOOD:

Rinse the clams and mussels*, peel and devein* the shrimp, cut the fish into 1-inch chunks, and cut lobster meat into ½-inch pieces.

TO PREPARE THE SAUCE:

Heat the oil in a heavy saucepan. Add in the ham and cook for a few

*See Kitchen Notes

155

minutes before adding the vegetables (except the okra). Stir frequently until the onions are clear and the peppers are soft.

Cut the lemon into thin slices, then cut again so no skin piece is larger than ½ inch long. Add the lemon and all the other remaining ingredients to the pot. Bring the mixture to a slow boil, reduce heat, and simmer gently for 30 minutes. Stir periodically to prevent scorching.

To assemble and cook:

In a large shallow pan (wok or Dutch oven) arrange the seafood, beginning with the fish. Nestle the clams and mussels, hinge side down, between pieces of fish. Finish with the shrimp, scallops, and lobster meat.

Add a cup of water and cook on medium heat for 10 minutes.

Add in the Creole sauce and continue cooking until the mix is boiling and the clams and mussels are all open. Stir gently once or twice during the cooking.

Lobster Sauté

THIS CLASSIC IS EASY to prepare. We recommend drawn butter for its good behavior in the sauté pan.

FOR EACH PERSON, ALLOW:

6 ounces fresh lobster meat

2 tablespoons drawn butter*   *Dash of paprika*
2 tablespoons dry white wine   *Salt, to taste*

Clean lobster meat by removing sand vein and tendons. Cut into bite-sized chunks.

Heat the butter, add in the lobster meat, and cook for a few minutes on medium to low heat until lobster meat is quite hot.

Sprinkle with paprika, then pour in the wine. Shake the pan back and forth to allow the wine to mix well with the butter and coat the chunks of meat.

For an extra rich, decadent sauce, drop in a few dollops of unmelted butter, turn off the heat, then shake the pan until the butter melts.

Taste for salt, then remove to small shallow bowls. Garnish with lemon wedges and fresh parsley.

Paella

Serves 8

THE PRIDE OF SPANISH PORT TOWNS, paella is a masterpiece you can create at home. It is actually named for the dish that is traditionally cooked in a large, round, heavy skillet. To simplify matters, I prefer to cook it in the oven, using ingredients readily available in New England.

Allow plenty of time for assembly or even better, get your guests to help. Once it's in the oven, you have over an hour to recuperate from your efforts and savor the anticipation!

Use only the freshest ingredients and as always, inspect the shellfish carefully discarding any open clams, or those with broken shells.*

1 pound haddock, skinned   *16 mussels in the shell*
½ pound scallops   *16 littleneck clams in the shell*
¼ pound lobster meat   *½ pound boneless chicken*
*½ pound shrimp, peeled & deveined**
*2 small squid, cleaned & cut into rings (keep tentacles)**
½ pound spicy sausage, chorico or linguica

2 cups rice   *2 tablespoons diced pimento*
2 tablespoons olive oil   *1 cup frozen peas*
2 tablespoons minced garlic   *1 teaspoon salt*
1 onion, diced   *½ teaspoon black pepper*
4 cups hot water   *1 cup white wine*
Several strands saffron or ¼ teaspoon turmeric

*See Kitchen Notes

TO PREPARE THE RICE:

Stir the saffron or turmeric into the hot water.

Heat a large saucepan, add in the olive oil, then the garlic and onion. Cook until the onion is clear.

Add the rice and cook for a few minutes, stirring frequently.

Add in the hot water, cover, bring it to a boil then reduce heat and cook for 15 minutes. Turn off the heat, add the salt and pepper, and let the rice sit for 5 minutes.

Brush a 10-by-13 heavy baking dish with olive oil and turn the rice into it, spreading it out to cool.

If you plan to cook the paella right away, you may add the seafood in while the rice is hot. Otherwise, wait until the rice is at least room temperature.

TO PREPARE THE MEAT AND SEAFOOD:

Cut the haddock into 1-inch chunks, peel the shrimp and rinse the clams and mussels well. If the scallops are large, cut them in half. Cut the lobster meat into ½-inch pieces. Cut the sausage to ¼-inch slices. Return the meats and seafood to the refrigerator until needed.

TO ASSEMBLE THE PAELLA:

Begin by placing the haddock, scallops, chicken, sausage, squid, and lobster meat on the rice. Using a spoon, tuck the pieces into the rice.

Sprinkle the peas and pimentos over the mix, also working them in with the spoon.

Arrange the clams and mussels on the top, hinge side imbedded in the rice.

Finally, add the shrimp, snugging them in enough that they will show, but not cook too quickly. Cover and refrigerate until needed or go directly to the next step.

TO COOK THE PAELLA:

Preheat oven to 400° F.

Pour the cup of wine over the paella and cover it well with foil.

Cooking time will vary according to the temperature of the dish when it goes into the oven. If you put it in warm, check it after 45 minutes.

If the dish has been chilled before cooking, allow it to cook for an hour and 15 minutes then check for doneness. If the clams and mussels are all opened, and the haddock is pure white and flaky, the paella is ready to eat. If not, return to the oven and check at 10-minute intervals.

The Winter Catch

WINTER BRINGS MANY CHANGES to the Cape & Islands waters. Lobstermen from Menemsha on the western edge of the Vineyard to Provincetown at the outermost tip of the Cape all bring in their traps for the winter. The weirs are pulled and stacked on Harding's Beach in Chatham. Rods and reels used for bluefish and striped bass are in basements for overhauling. Even the floating docks which fill the harbors like are pulled out of the water. Winter rules, and local fishermen have learned how to cope. Still, fishing does not come to a halt.

Even in our days of global warming we can't count the number of days the cod fishing boats have to break the ice in the harbors to get out to fish. To check to see if any of our boats are out, we only have to look for a broken trail through the icebound harbor, and we know. On windy days, the large boats that managed to get out have one person just breaking ice off the boat's riggings with a hatchet. Because the ice makes it top-heavy, a boat covered with frozen sea spray easily can capsize.

As bad as all that sounds, there is nothing like the pride on a fisherman's face when he comes home with a good catch in the face of that adversity. In fact, rarely do we hear any fisherman complain about the weather in winter. About the wind, maybe; about a lack of fish, definitely; but never about the temperature. Sometimes they report that the temperature is warmer on the ocean than it is on land. The ocean might drop to 34° Fahrenheit, a warming effect on a day in the teens.

There is nothing like the pride on a fisherman's face when he comes home with a good catch in the face of this season's adversity.

161

Shellfishing also continues in winter. Clam flats are workable unless covered with ice. Most towns set temperature minimums to protect young shellfish from freezing. If the air temperature drops below 30°, the diggers have to just watch and wait. Don't tell the warden, but we have known fishermen to turn their thermometers toward the sun to help boost it a few precious degrees. I often chuckle at how people will say how cold it looks on the water, when they are sitting in cars with the heat on high.

Those fishermen you see out in the elements are often sweating from the exertion of clamming. I have done it, raking for clams out in Stage Harbor, back to the wind, eyes watering from the cold. But if your waders are watertight, and your long-johns dry, you really don't mind the weather. And that hot coffee surely works when you hit the shore!

Another offshore fishery that thrives in winter is sea scalloping. Cape Cod Bay produces some great sea scallops during winter. Large and tender, these are high quality scallops. Rave as we do about bay scallops, dayboat sea scallops can be nearly as good, though different in taste. Some people actually like them better, because they are not as sweet.

The key to a good sea scallop has always been the length of time that a boat is out to sea. The large boats from New Bedford, Gloucester, and elsewhere are out catching scallops for 7 to 10 days per trip. Those scallops are often old before they even hit the dock. Mainly out of ports on the North side of the Cape, only a few local boats get involved in this activity. Provincetown, Wellfleet, Orleans, Dennis, Barnstable, and Sandwich all have harbors that might see landings of sea scallops, and these smallboat scallopers working out of our ports are out for a maximum of 24 hours. So, the quality of their catch is terrific.

Unfortunately, another recent "miracle" affecting scallop quality is a chemical approved by the FDA to treat scallops with fresh water. While this "soaking" adds weight to the scallops, it also preserves them, giving them a greater shelf-life. That means that processors can take 100 pounds of scallops, add the chemical, soak them overnight, and legally have 125 pounds of scallops for sale! Of course, they have to post a sign stating that these are "Scallop product, 25% water added".

Rave as we often do about bay scallops, dayboat sea scallops can be nearly as good, though different in taste.

Guess how often that happens. How many restaurant diners see "scallop product newburg" on the menu? But how many diners have noticed scallops just don't taste the way that they used to? Or that there is a funny aftertaste, a little burn on their tongue after eating scallops. Please don't stop eating scallops. Just be sure to ask if they are processed or "dry". "Dry scallops" are the new lingo for real scallops, the way they always were: natural and fresh from the sea!

Scallops are also the only shellfish to have a patron saint. St. James, the apostle, wore scallop shells as his personal emblem. Pilgrims to his shrine during the Middle Ages wore the shells in tribute. The famous scallop dish, *Coquille Saint-Jacques*, derives its name from him.

Winter also brings an added advantage to local seafood as the quality of our fish reaches its pinnacle for the year. The simple reason is that Mother Nature acts like a refrigerator, keeping the day's catch cold through every phase of its journey to us. While our own fishermen always bring ice on their boats to preserve the quality of their catch, this is not true of all fishermen. So, winter weather helps to maintain quality of all the fish that is landed throughout the Cape & Islands, and the shelf-life of fresh fish increases by 2 or 3 days when the weather is frosty.

This is also very true of shellfish. Mussels, for example, only stay alive for 2 or 3 days in the summer. The warm weather actually decreases oxygen levels of inshore waters. Mussels taken in winter live for 5 or 6 days. Shellfish also are much fuller in the winter. Just as the locals do, they fatten-up in the winter. (Not enough exercise, I guess.) Twelve quahogs shucked in winter will yield 1 pint of meat, while that same number of quahogs shucked in summer will yield about ¾ of a pint.

Pollution along inshore waters is also significantly lessened in the winter. With our population reduced, there is less stress on the ecosystem throughout the Cape & Islands. Quality just can't be surpassed in winter.

The biggest problem, though, is that we do see many days in winter when fishing is just plain impossible. Fishermen never plan vacations. The wind will do that for them. In fact, the fishermen are more in touch with the weather than anyone else I know. Farmers are affected by it.

Scallops are also the only shellfish to have a patron saint. St. James, the apostle, wore scallop shells as his personal emblem.

People who work outdoors are affected by it. But fishermen are really in touch with it. They listen to broadcasts from the National Oceanic and Atmospheric Administration throughout the day on marine frequencies, and they know from wind direction whether to expect rain or sunshine.

If you want to know tomorrow's weather, you're far better off asking a fisherman than a weatherman. The outdoors is their office! Fishermen can read clouds and wave-chops and wind speeds the way most businesspeople read faxes and financial reports. Fishermen commune with the natural world, much like our Native American predecessors. And in the winter, more than the rest of the year, that is a matter of life and death.

Winter is also chowder season. Somehow the thought of a thick, creamy chowder just doesn't work for you when you're in someplace sunny, like Florida. Or Phoenix. Or California. But when you're chilled to the bone, and it's damp and raw outside, there are few more welcoming thoughts than a tasty clam or fish chowder waiting for you inside.

I said there are *few*. While there are dozens (if not hundreds) of recipes out there for chowder, there are a handful of key rules that any *good* chowder must follow. Good fresh fish and/or clams certainly are near the top of that list. Fresh spuds are somewhere in that same are. But the Number One Rule for a great chowder is plenty of onion!

Start with butter or margarine or oil or lard or pork rind. Whatever. And use fish stock or water or (shudder) chicken broth. Whatever. But you must plan on plenty of onion sautéed first. *That* is the flavor binder, the Number One key to a good chowder. If you're going to be stingy with the onion, then you might just as well open up a can of soup!

Winter is definitely a season of beauty throughout the Cape & Islands. While most people visit here in the warm weather, their images of this peninsula and islands are shaped by summertime activities; however, the real Cape Cod, the real Nantucket, the real Martha's Vineyard are far easier to find in winter than in any other season.

While there are dozens – if not hundreds – of recipes out there for chowder, there are but a handful of key rules that any good chowder must follow.

A Winter Menu

Appetizer
Portuguese Stuffed Mussels
Wrapped Shrimp with Basil & Prosciutto
Shrimp & Artichoke Hearts Wrapped with Bacon
Crabmeat Patrice
Terry's Clams Casino
Smoked Salmon & Caviar Pizza
Shrimp Mousse in Filo Packets
Crab Stuffed Mushroom Caps

Soup
Spicy Seafood Stew
New England Fish Chowder
Dairy-Free Clam Chowder
Billi-bi

Entrées
Scrod Oreganata
Newburg Sauce
Seafood Newburg en Casserole
Mussels Marinara
Baked Swordfish with Rosemary Wine Butter
Sea Scallops Marsala

Sea Scallops Provençal
Creamed Finnan Haddie on Toast
Ocean Catfish Cacciatore
Baked Whole Haddock with Seafood Stuffing
Seafood Lasagna with Tomato Basil Bêchamel
Cod Steaks with Sundried Tomato Butter
Cuban Mahi-Mahi Dinner
Baked Scrod with Mushroom Miso Sauce
Seafood Mornay

Portuguese Stuffed Mussels

Yields 50 stuffed mussels

THOUGH THIS IS A SOMEWHAT time-consuming recipe, it can easily be broken down into manageable segments. For example, the preparation could be done on one day; then, the assembling finished, the next. In addition, you can freeze stuffed mussels and bake them as needed.

*3 pounds mussels in their shell**
2 cups bread bits
2 tablespoons olive oil
1 tablespoon garlic, chopped fine
4 tablespoons butter or margarine
½ cup onion, diced ¼-inch cubes
1 cup reserved broth from mussels

2 plum tomatoes
3 ounces chourico (Portuguese hot sausage)
¼ teaspoon red pepper
1 tablespoon parsley, chopped
1 tablespoon cilantro, chopped

In a 10-quart pot, bring 1 cup of water to a boil and add the mussels. Cover and allow the mussels to steam for 6 or 7 minutes. Check to be sure all the shells are opened. If not, resume cooking until they are. Drain the cooking liquid and reserve for later use.

Once the mussels are cool enough to handle, remove them from their shells, de-beard them and rinse in a large bowl of cold water to wash away any remaining grit. Lift the mussels out of the water and set them in the refrigerator until they are chilled. Cold mussels are firmer, easier to cut, and less likely to break up in the stuffing mix.

Because you will need 50 half shells to stuff, sort through the shells and select enough mid-sized ones. Rinse well and refrigerate until needed.

*See Kitchen Notes

167

To make the bread bits:

The object here is not to create bread crumbs, but pieces the size of a commercial stuffing mix.

Preheat the oven to 350º F.

Take a 6-inch segment of Italian bread (stale is fine), tear it into pieces, then put them on a cookie pan to bake. After 5 minutes, remove them from the oven, break down the larger pieces, and repeat until all the bread is crispy and reduced to very coarse crumbs.

To prepare the stuffing:

Heat a 10-inch skillet, then add the oil and butter. Once the butter is melted, add the onion and garlic, cooking on a medium heat until the onions are clear. Remove seeds and pulp from the tomatoes, then cut into a ¼-inch dice. Add the tomatoes and the chourico to the onions, then cook for a few minutes. Pour 1 cup of the reserved broth into the skillet. Simmer this mix gently for 10 minutes to allow the flavors to blend.

Lay the cooled mussel meats in a row upon a cutting board and cut them with a long, sharp knife. The pieces should be about the size of large peas. After the initial pass of the knife down the row of mussels, go back and re-cut those that may have been cut lengthwise. Be careful not to overcut, or you will soon have a rather unappetizing mess in front of you.

Add the herbs into the pot, stir briefly, then add the mussels.

Put the bread bits into a large bowl and add the mussel mix, stirring carefully, just until all the ingredients are combined. Let the mixture cool for 10 minutes, then stuff the shells with one tablespoon of stuffing mix in each.

Preheat the oven to 400° F. Bake for 5 or 6 minutes until the mussels are lightly-browned on top. Avoid overcooking so that they do not dry out.

Wrapped Shrimp
with Basil & Prosciutto

Serves 6

YOU CAN NEVER MISS when you serve shrimp as an *hors d'oeuvre*. This complete blend of flavors gives it star appeal!

36 large shrimp, uncooked, deveined & peeled, with tail on

36 whole fresh basil leaves
18 thin slices proscuitto

FOR THE HORSERADISH DIPPING SAUCE:
½ cup horseradish
½ cup mayonnaise

TO PREPARE THE SHRIMP:

Cut the proscuitto in half lengthwise.

Leaving the tail exposed, wrap each shrimp: first, with a basil leaf; then, with the proscuitto. Skewer each with a toothpick to hold in place.

Arrange the shrimp in a shallow baking dish and cook at 400° F for 10 to 12 minutes.

Garnish with lemon wedges and fresh basil leaves and serve with dipping sauce,

TO PREPARE THE HORSERADISH DIPPING SAUCE:

Blend the two ingredients and refrigerate until needed.

Shrimp & Artichoke Hearts
Wrapped with Bacon

THESE MAKE WONDERFUL HORS D'OEUVRES for holiday entertaining. If you wish, you can make them a day ahead, then bake as needed.

Allow 4 or 5 medium shrimp per person

1 package of frozen artichoke hearts
Bacon strips, partially-cooked and cut in half

Preheat the oven to 400° F.

Thaw the artichoke hearts and cut lengthwise into quarters.

Fold the shrimp around the artichoke heart, wrap with bacon and secure with a toothpick.

Place in a shallow baking dish and bake until the bacon is crisp. They will probably take a total of 10 minutes, but should be checked and turned over after 5 minutes.

Crabmeat Patrice

ANOTHER FINE ADDITION to your repertoire of delicious holiday appetizers!

8 ounces cream cheese (room temperature)
6 to 8 ounces crabmeat   *¼ teaspoon salt*
1 tablespoon milk   *Dash of white pepper*
½ teaspoon horseradish   *¼ cup almonds, sliced*

Preheat the oven to 375° F.

Combine everything together except the almonds, then spread the mixture in a 6-inch round, shallow baking dish (or the equivalent). Sprinkle the almonds on top and bake for 15 minutes.

Serve hot or cold in the baking dish with Melba toast, crackers, or crudites.

Terry's Clams Casino

Serves 6

THANKS TO TERRY SHEPHERD for this refreshing recipe.

36 littleneck clams, rinsed well

1 clove of garlic, minced
1 small onion, diced into ¼-inch pieces
½ green pepper, diced fine
5 strips of bacon, cut into 1-inch pieces

Mix the cut vegetables together in a small bowl and set aside.

Open the clams*, free the meat from the bottom shell, and place them on the half shell in a shallow dish suitable for broiling.

Place about 1 tablespoon of the stuffing on each clam, then top with bacon.

Cook them under the broiler until the bacon is crisp and brown.

See Kitchen Notes

Smoked Salmon & Caviar
Pizza

Serves 4 to 6

THIS VARIATION IS WONDERFUL either as an appetizer, or as an elegant lunch fare.

FOR THE PIZZA DOUGH AND CRUST:
See Gourmet Pizza with White Clam Sauce *on page 25.*

FOR THE TOPPING:

¼ pound smoked salmon (either lox or dry-smoked salmon)

8 ounces Boursin herbed cheese
2 tablespoons caviar

TO PREPARE THE PIZZA CRUST:

Make dough according to the recipe for the Gourmet Pizza with White Clam Sauce, then follow the baking instructions. Once this crust has been baked, remove it from the oven and allow it to cool.

TO PREPARE THE PIZZA:

Preheat the oven to 350° F.

Spread the Boursin onto the cooled, baked pizza crust.

Cut the smoked fish into small slices and place on top of the cheese.

Heat the pizza for 10 minutes.

Dot the top of the pizza with caviar, then transfer to a serving platter, cut, and serve.

Shrimp Mousse
in Filo Packets

Yields 12 packets

YOU MAY SPEND an hour or two making these, but the grateful diners will polish them off in minutes. Make sure you *really* like the people you're cooking for; otherwise, serve cocktail franks and ketchup.

1 pound uncooked, medium shrimp, peeled and deveined

1 cup heavy cream	*½ teaspoon oregano*
1 egg yolk	*1 box filo dough, defrosted*
¼ teaspoon white pepper	*¾ cup melted butter*
¼ teaspoon nutmeg	*Fresh ground black pepper*
1 cup grated Romano cheese (fresh grated if possible)	

TO MAKE THE MOUSSE:

Pass the shrimp through a meat grinder using the fine blade. (If a grinder is not available, lay the shrimp out on a cutting board and use a long sharp knife to mince the shrimp until it is the consistency of ground meat. A food processor will *not* work for this procedure.)

Put the shrimp into a bowl and sprinkle with the white pepper, oregano, nutmeg, and half of the Romano cheese.

Mix the egg yolk and cream together in a cup, then pour over the shrimp. Mix well. Refrigerate until needed.

TO MAKE THE PACKETS:

Assemble the following next to a clean, dry work space: a sheet pan,

Filo dough can be difficult to work with, but it's definitely not impossible. If you are a beginning cook, just give yourself a little extra time and be patient. You can master this.
– Sometimes the first sheet will be

melted butter, pastry brush, pepper mill, Romano cheese, the filo dough, and the shrimp mixture.

Open the filo out onto a clean, dry section of counter with an equal-sized space right next to it. If you think work will be slow, or you will be interrupted, have a clean, damp dish towel handy to lay over the dough to prevent drying.

Separate one sheet of filo from the rest and lay it out onto the counter. Working quickly, brush the surface with melted butter, paying particular care to the edges. Sprinkle with fresh ground black pepper and Romano cheese. Repeating the process for each, lay a second and a third sheet on top.

Cut the filo into 12 rectangles.

Lay one rectangle diagonally across another and put 1 tablespoon of shrimp mix in the center. Working one corner at a time, bring the filo up to cover the shrimp mix, folding the edges back slightly so you end up with a little pouch surrounding the shrimp, and a number of pastry edges pointing up and out, like a little fountain on top. It's fine to have a little of the shrimp exposed.

As you complete each packet, place it on the sheet pan. Continue until you run out of filling.

Refrigerate the appetizers until you need them.

Bake in a 350° F oven for 10 to 12 minutes or until edges are browned. Shrimp packets may be served hot or warm.

dry. If it cracks when you pull it off the pile, throw it out and go to the next one.

– Using a damp towel to cover the dough you're not using at the moment can help. Just be sure it's not too wet or else water will turn the pastry to paste, and there's no fixing that.

– If the sheets stick together, run your hand under the one you're trying to lift.

– If the sheets tear as you use them, that's okay; you'll be adding more layers anyway.

Crab Stuffed Mushroom Caps

Yields 25 to 30

USE FRESH SWEET CRABMEAT, and this old standby will *never* lose its appeal.

½ pound fresh crabmeat
25 to 30 medium mushrooms
¾ cup bread crumbs
¾ cup Ritz cracker crumbs
1½ teaspoons paprika
½ teaspoon garlic salt
1 teaspoon dry mustard powder

¼ cup finely diced green pepper
¼ cup finely diced onion
¼ cup melted butter
3 tablespoon white wine
3 tablespoon lemon juice
1½ teaspoons Worcestershire sauce
Dash of Tabasco

Remove the stems from the mushrooms and wipe the caps with a damp paper towel. Set aside.

Mix the bread crumbs, cracker crumbs, paprika, garlic salt, and mustard powder in a medium bowl, then add the green peppers and onions.

Inspect the crabmeat for shell and cartilage, then add to the mixture.

In a measuring cup, mix the remaining ingredients and pour over the crabmeat mixture. Fold everything together, taking care not to break up the crabmeat chunks.

For each mushroom, take 1 tablespoon of the crab mixture, form it into a loosely packed ball, and mound it into the cap.

Place the mushrooms into a shallow, buttered baking dish.

Bake for 15 to 20 minutes at 400° F.

Spicy Seafood Stew

Serves 4 to 6

THIS RECIPE EVOLVED as a means of using the little packets of leftover seafood that always seemed to accumulate in our freezer. A few shrimp scampi, a lobster tail, and some scrod were the basis of our first version, but your own may vary according to the ingredients available to you. If you choose to follow the recipe below, but raw clams or mussels are not used, you may substitute bottled clam juice or seafood bouillion cubes for the broth.

2 tablespoons olive oil
2 cloves garlic, minced
1 onion, diced
1 medium potato, diced
1 stalk celery, diced
1 medium carrot, diced
1 leek, cut into ½-inch lengths
1 teaspoon thyme
1 tablespoon flour
1 15-ounce can tomato sauce
2 tablespoons lime juice

8 littleneck clams, rinsed well
8 small mussels, scrubbed and de-bearded*
¼ pound shrimp, shelled and deveined*
¼ pound scallops
½ pound firm white fish
¼ teaspoon black pepper
Dash of white pepper
¼ teaspoon crushed red pepper
1 tablespoon chopped parsley

Steam the mussels and clams in a medium saucepan using ½ cup of water.

Drain off the broth and set aside. Allow the shellfish to cool, then remove the meats from shells and reserve.

*See Kitchen Notes

In a small saucepan, cook the carrot and potato together in 1 cup of water. When the vegetables are cooked *al dente*, drain the cooking liquid into the container with the shellfish broth and set both the liquid and the vegetables aside.

Heat a large pot and add the oil.

Cook the garlic, onion, celery, and leek on medium heat, stirring occasionally, until the onions are clear.

Sprinkle the flour into the pot and cook, stirring for 3 or 4 minutes until it is well mixed.

Add the liquids reserved from the shellfish and vegetables. Stir well to ensure that the flour blends in without making lumps, then add all of the remaining ingredients *except* the fish and shellfish.

Simmer for 20 minutes, then add in the seafood.

From that point, the stew will need to cook another 15 minutes; however, it should not go too much longer as the fish could easily over-cook and break apart.

New England Fish Chowder

Serves 4

FOR THIS HEARTY CREAM SOUP choose a firm white fish, such as ocean catfish, monkfish, haddock, halibut, or cod.

5 slices of bacon, in ¼-inch pieces	*3 tablespoons flour*
½ cup onion, diced	*3 cups whole milk or cream*
¼ cup celery, diced	*¼ teaspoon thyme*
1½ pounds white fish	*2 tablespoons oil, margarine, or*
1½ pounds potatoes	*the bacon drippings*

Remove skin and bones from the fish and rinse.

In a medium-sized skillet, bring 1 cup of water to a boil and add the thyme. Lay the fish in the water, cover, and simmer gently for 7 to 10 minutes. When the fish has cooked, drain and reserve the broth to use in the chowder.

Dice the potatoes into ½-inch cubes and cook in a small saucepan with 1 cup of water. When the potatoes are tender, drain the water into the fish broth, then set it and the potatoes aside.

In a 4-quart saucepan, cook the bacon until crisp and remove from the pan with a slotted spoon. Using the bacon drippings or 2 table-spoons of oil or butter, sauté the onions and celery until tender.

Add the flour to the pan with the onions and celery, then cook for a few minutes on medium heat, stirring to prevent scorching.

Slowly add the broth mixture, stirring with a wire whisk to work out lumps. Allow this to cook for a few minutes, then add the milk and stir to blend.

Add in the potatoes, the bacon, and the fish, then heat the chowder until it is piping hot. Once the fish and potatoes have been added, stir very gently to prevent the fish from breaking apart. Also, be careful not to let the chowder become so hot that the milk will curdle.

Though the chowder is now ready to serve, many locals feel it is better the second day. If you can wait that long, allow it to cool, then refrigerate until the next day.

Dairy-Free Clam Chowder

Serves 4 to 6

THIS RECIPE WAS DEVELOPED for a friend who was allergic to milk, but still very fond of clams. It is delicious as presented here; however, you could easily add milk or cream at the end to please any traditionalists.

4 tablespoons vegetable oil
4 tablespoons flour
2 onions, diced
1 pint of chopped quahogs, sea clams, or both

5 medium potatoes
1 cup of clam broth
1 cup of water
¼ teaspoon white pepper

Peel and dice the potatoes. In a small saucepan, boil them with 2 cups of water until they are soft. Allow them to cool slightly, then remove about a third of the potatoes and all of the cooking liquid to a blender. Process them until it is a smooth purée. Set this and the remaining cooked potatoes aside.

In a 4-quart saucepan, heat the oil, add in the onions, and cook on medium heat until they are clear.

Add the flour and cook, stirring constantly, for 5 minutes.

Slowly pour in the broth and water, stirring with a wire whisk to eliminate the lumps. Sprinkle the white pepper over the mixture and allow it to come to the boiling point.

Carefully add the clams, stir them in, reduce the heat to low and simmer for 10 to 15 minutes, stirring occasionally. The clams should firm-up, but still be tender. Remember, overcooking will make them tough.

The potatoes and their purée may be added now. Allow the chowder to heat thoroughly.

Ladle into bowls, then garnish with chopped parsley, scallions, or both.

Billi-bi

Serves 4

BILLI-BI, A RICH, CREAM-BASED MUSSEL SOUP, originated in France. This may not be the pedigreed version, but it makes fine use of the lowly local bivalve.

2 pounds mussels in the shell

Linguine, serving for one
4 tablespoons butter
½ cup jullienned red onions
½ cup sliced mushrooms
3 tablespoons flour
3 tablespoons sherry

2 cups light cream or milk
2 cups mussel broth
¼ teaspoon white pepper
Salt, to taste
2 tablespoons sliced scallion greens
Paprika, for garnish

Clean and steam the mussels.*

Reserve 2 cups of the cooking broth. Remove the meats from the shells and refrigerate until needed.

Linguine for one would be the uncooked pasta enough to fill a circle ½ inch in diameter. Break the pasta into 2-inch pieces and cook according to package directions.

Drain the pasta and hold in ice water until you need it for the soup.

In a 3-quart sauce pan, sauté the onions and mushrooms in butter until they are quite soft.

Add in the flour and cook for 2 minutes before adding in the mussel broth. Stir with a wire whisk to prevent lumps.

*See Kitchen Notes

Add in the cream, cooked linguine, mussels, and sherry, then cook on low heat until the soup is steaming hot. Do not allow it to come to the boil as it will curdle.

Taste and adjust the seasonings.

Ladle into bowls, garnish with scallions and paprika.

Scrod Oreganata

Serves 4

IT REALLY DOESN'T GET ANY EASIER! Serve with a side of pasta marinara and a green salad for a hearty, healthy dinner.

2 pounds scrod fillet

FOR THE CRUMB MIX:

1 cup seasoned bread crumbs *1 teaspoon basil*
½ cup Parmesan cheese *¼ teaspoon salt*
1 teaspoon oregano *¼ teaspoon black pepper*

Preheat the oven to 400° F.

Combine the dry ingredients to make crumb mix.

Remove skin from the scrod*, rinse the fillet quickly in cold, running water, cut into portion sizes, and pat dry with a paper towel.

Lightly coat fish with oil or melted butter.

Sprinkle both sides of fish generously with crumbs and place in shallow baking dish.

Bake for 10 to 12 minutes.

Check the thickest part of the fillet to be sure it is cooked through. Serve immediately.

*See Kitchen Notes

Newburg Sauce

Yiels 1½ cups

NEWBURG SAUCE CAN BE USED in a variety of ways with seafood. An enduring favorite is a casserole of mixed fish and shellfish, topped with sauce, baked, then served with toast points. The sauce can be used as a topping for any broiled fish, combined with shrimp or lobster for an elegant entrée, or used with crêpes for a luncheon. Regardless of how you choose to use it, this sauce creates a hearty winter dish.

1 tablespoon butter or margarine	*1 cup light cream*
2 tablespoons flour	*½ teaspoon Worcestershire sauce*
2 tablespoons sherry	*2 to 3 drops Tabasco*
1 teaspoon paprika	*Dash of salt*

Melt the butter in a small saucepan. Add the flour and cook, stirring frequently, for 3 minutes. In a small bowl, combine the sherry, paprika, Worcestershire sauce, Tabasco, and salt. Add this mixture into the melted butter and flour, stirring with a wire whisk to blend. Almost immediately, add the cream in a slow steady stream, whisking at the same time to prevent lumps from forming. Continue stirring over medium heat until sauce thickens, then reduce heat to a very low temperature and cook for another 5 minutes.

The sauce is now ready to serve, or to be refrigerated until needed.

Seafood Newburg
en Casserole

THIS RECIPE SERVES SIX PEOPLE, but it can easily be multiplied to feed a crowd. You may wish to add toast points just before serving, or to have them available on the side. In any case . . . *Bon Appétit!*

> *1½ pounds of scrod or other white fish*
> *½ pound scallops*
> *½ pound uncooked shrimp, peeled and deveined**
> *6 ounces lobster meat*
> *3 cups* Newburg Sauce

Arrange the fish, scallops, and shrimp in a 9-by-12 baking dish. Pour a ½ cup of water into the pan and cover it with a lid or foil. Bake for 20 to 30 minutes. Check for doneness by flaking the fish with a fork or by cutting into a scallop to be sure it is white throughout.

When the fish is fully cooked, carefully drain the cooking juice, and save it to add to the sauce.

Remove the cartilage and sand vein from the lobster meat, cut into bite-size pieces, then arrange on top of the other fish.

Stir the fish broth into the sauce, then pour it over the fish mixture so that it covers the seafood well. This may be baked immediately or refrigerated until needed.

If you are cooking it immediately, the uncovered casserole needs 15 to 20 minutes in a 375° F oven. If it is taken from the refrigerator, it needs about 30 minutes to get the center hot and make the edges bubble.

*See Kitchen Notes

Mussels Marinara

Serves 4 to 6

IN MY FAMILY there are two schools of thought on the subject of mussels in a sauce such as this. My husband thinks the mussels should be cooked *in* the sauce, *in* their shells, and served over linguine, just like that! His argument is that the flavor produced by such a method should not be sacrificed for tidiness. While his view has certain merits, I still maintain that shells *in* a tomato sauce are a messy affair and may try the patience of some diners.

As a domestic compromise, I offer both versions of the recipe so that you may decide which method suits you according to the delicacy or gusto of the people you will be feeding.

4 tablespoons olive oil	*½ teaspoon oregano*
½ cup onion, chopped	*½ teaspoon basil*
½ cup green pepper, chopped	*10 black olives, sliced*
½ cup mushrooms, sliced	*1 15-ounce can tomato sauce*
2 cloves garlic, diced fine	*¼ cup red wine*
4 pounds mussels in their shells*	*Salt and pepper to taste*
Linguine	

In a large skillet, sauté all the vegetables in the olive oil until they are tender and the onions are clear. Add in the remaining ingredients (*except* the mussels) and simmer gently for about 15minutes. Add in the mussels, either uncooked *in* the shell, or cooked *out* of the shell. If you have

*See Kitchen Notes

chosen to use the mussels in the shell, cook for about 15 minutes or until the shells open. If you have chosen to use the pre-cooked mussels removed from the shell, cook only 5 or 10 minutes in the hot sauce.

Prepare the pasta according to directions on package.

Pour the sauce over steaming hot linguine and serve with plenty of napkins!

Baked Swordfish
with Rosemary Wine Butter

Serves 4

2 pounds swordfish

FOR THE ROSEMARY WINE BUTTER:

1 tablespoon fresh rosemary, stems removed*, chopped

6 tablespoons melted butter	*1 teaspoon salt*
¼ cup white wine	*½ teaspoon pepper*
1 cup flour	*Lemon to garnish*

*Reserve 2 inches from the tip of each sprig for a garnish

Preheat oven to 400° F.

In a small saucepan, simmer the melted butter, rosemary, and wine for 5 minutes to blend the flavors.

Meanwhile, in a flat bowl or pie plate, mix the flour, salt and pepper. Lay the fish pieces in the flour to coat both sides, then remove them to a shallow, buttered baking dish.

Ladle the rosemay wine butter mix over the fish and bake for 15 minutes.

Check for doneness by piercing the thickest part of the fish with a small sharp knife. If the knife meets resistance, continue to cook. If it goes in like butter, the fish is ready to serve.

Garnish with rosemary sprigs and lemon rounds.

Sea Scallops Marsala

Serves 4

HERE IS A QUICK AND EASY preparation for scallops!

1½ to 2 pounds of scallops *¼ cup bread crumbs*
½ cup Marsala *Black pepper to taste*
¼ cup melted butter *Swiss cheese to cover scallops*

Preheat the oven to 400° F.

Arrange the scallops in shallow baking dish so that they fit either in a single layer, or no deeper than two layers. Drizzle the Marsala over them according to taste. Follow with a little melted butter, freshly ground black pepper, and a layer of Swiss cheese. Sprinkle the top with a dusting of bread crumbs.

Bake for 15 to 20 minutes, or until the edges are bubbling, and the top is a light golden color.

SEASONED BY THE SEA

Sea Scallops Provençal

T HIS IS A "BEST SELLER" in Swan River Restaurants.

1½ to 2 pounds of scallops

FOR THE BREADING MIX:
¾ cup bread crumbs
¾ cup flour
¼ cup Parmesan cheese
2 tablespoons parsley, chopped

FOR THE GARLIC BUTTER MIX:
¼ cup butter, melted
4 tablespoons white wine
2 teaspoons garlic, chopped fine

Preheat the oven to 400° F.

Mix the breading ingredients in a spacious bowl. Add the scallops and toss until they are completely coated. Lift the scallops out of the crumb mix and place them in a baking dish in a single, snug layer. Sprinkle a little of the crumb mix on top of the scallops, then drizzle with the garlic butter.

Bake for 15 to 20 minutes. To check for doneness, cut into one of the scallops to be sure it is opaque in the center. Be careful not to over-cook them, or they will become tough and dry.

Creamed Finnan Haddie
on Toast

Serves 4

THERE ARE MANY VARIETIES of smoked haddock on the market today. The most authentic still comes from Scotland and can be distinguished from impostors by its mellow golden color. The quick-smoked type, usually cod, has a rather garish yellow glow. Either way, this is a very satisfying traditional dish.

1½ pounds finnan haddie	*Dash of white pepper*
2 cups milk or light cream	*Salt, to taste*
4 tablespoons butter	*8 slices bread, for toast*
6 tablespoons flour	*Fresh chopped parsley, for garnish*

Cut finnan haddie into several chunks and place it in a saucepan. Cover with water and bring to the boil. Immediately reduce heat and simmer for 30 to 40 minutes until the fish is tender and flakes easily.

Lift the fish out of the water and lay it on a flat surface. Reserve 2 cups of the cooking liquid.

When the fish is cool enough to handle, break it into bite-sized chunks, inspecting carefully for bones. Set aside.

In a saucepan, melt the butter, add the flour, and cook together on medium heat for 5 minutes, stirring frequently.

Slowly add in the fish stock, stirring with a wire whisk to eliminate lumps. Cook for a few minutes and, as the sauce begins to thicken, whisk in the cream. Continue cooking on a low heat, stirring constantly to keep the sauce smooth. Do not allow it to boil or the sauce will curdle.

When the sauce is very hot, add in the chunks of fish and continue to cook on low heat until it is hot throughout.

Test for seasoning, adding salt if needed.

Serve on a slice of toast, with toast points on the side.

The traditional garnish includes chopped hard boiled eggs. We prefer fresh chopped parsley.

Ocean Catfish Cacciatore

Serves 4

HAVE YOU EVER WONDERED what to do with ocean catfish? It might well be the ugliest fish in the sea, but it tastes great and has the perfect texture for this hearty preparation. Serve it with thick slices of garlic bread to sop up the juices, or else with a mound of steaming risotto on the side. Then, again, if ocean cat is just too ugly to suit your tastes, sea bass or halibut would make fine substitutes in this dish. Whatever your preference, *Buon appetito!*

2 pounds ocean catfish	*1 cup sliced mushrooms*
2 ripe tomatoes, in 1-inch chunks	*1 teaspoon dried oregano*
1 green pepper, coarsely diced	*½ teaspoon salt*
1 medium onion, in thin wedges	*Fresh ground black pepper, to taste*
2 cloves of garlic, minced	*3 tablespoons olive oil*

Heat a small sauté pan, add the olive oil, then the garlic and mushrooms. Cook for 3 or 4 minutes, stirring or tossing the pan frequently. Set aside.

Preheat oven to 400° F. Brush the bottom of a shallow baking dish with olive oil. Arrange the fish in the pan and spread the tomatoes, peppers, onions and seasonings over them. Top with sautéed mushrooms and garlic. Cover with a lid or foil and bake for 25 to 30 minutes.

Check for doneness. If it is opaque and flakes easily, it is done. If not, return to the oven and cook for a few more minutes.

Baked Whole Haddock
with Seafood Stuffing

Serves 4 to 6

WE ARE OFTEN ASKED to bring this dish to family Christmas or Thanksgiving dinner. Haddock is considered by some to be "Cape Cod turkey." Select a 4 or 5 pound fish and ask your fishmonger to remove the bones, fins and head. Leave the head on if you'd like to get a rise out of the kids; adults would probably agree that it's much tidier and visually appealing without the head. Cod or pollock make ideal substitutes if haddock is not available.

4 to 5 pound whole fish, cleaned.

4 ounces butter	*¼ teaspoon Tabasco*
1 clove garlic, minced	*½ pound small shrimp, peeled & deveined*
1 onion, diced	*½ pound scallops, coarsely chopped*
½ cup white wine	*½ green pepper, in ¼-inch pieces*
1 teaspoon salt	*2 tablespoons fresh chopped parsley*
1 tablespoon lemon juice	*½ teaspoon black pepper*
2 teaspoons Worcestershire	*3 cups poultry stuffing crumbs*

Put the crumbs into a large bowl, add 1 cup boiling water, mix and set aside.

Using half the butter, sauté the garlic, onion and peppers until the onion is clear. Remove from the pan.

Using the remaining butter, sauté the shrimp and scallops for 4 or 5 minutes. Turn off the heat and add in all the remaining ingredients, except for the crumbs. Stir to mix, then pour over the crumbs. Mix well. If you will be cooking the fish at a later time, cool the stuffing before proceeding to the next step.

Lay the fish on a buttered sheet pan. Fill the body cavity with the stuffing and cover lightly with foil. At this point, you can cook the fish, or refrigerate to cook at your convenience.

Bake in a 400° F oven for 30 or 40 minutes.

Cooking times will vary depending on individual ovens, how much is in the oven, and the temperature of the fish when you begin cooking. Test for doneness by cutting into the thickest part of the flesh to see if it is opaque and flakes easily.

Garnish with plenty of fresh parsley and lemon wedges.

Seafood Lasagna
with Tomato Basil Bêchamel

Serves 8

1 pound uncooked medium shrimp, peeled and deveined*
¾ pound scallops   ½ pound lobster meat

2 tablespoons olive oil   2 pounds ricotta cheese
¼ teaspoon dried basil   2 eggs
¼ teaspoon dried oregano   ¼ cup Parmesan cheese
¼ teaspoon black pepper   1 tablespoon fresh chopped parsley
1 one pound box lasagna   1 cup grated mozzarella cheese
1 quart marinara sauce

FOR THE BÊCHAMEL SAUCE:

4 tablespoons butter   2 tablespoons fresh chopped basil
6 tablespoons flour   Salt, to taste
1½ cup seafood stock**   ¼ teaspoon white pepper
1½ cup light cream   Pinch of nutmeg
3 tablespoons tomato purée

** Begin with the cooking juices from the shrimp and scallops. Add in
enough broth made with bouillon cubes for a total of 1½ cups.

TO COOK THE SEAFOOD:

Cut the shrimp, scallops, and lobster meat into chunks about ¾-
inch across. You want a piece that's big enough to taste, but not big
enough to make lumpy layers.

Heat the olive oil in a sauté pan and cook the shrimp and scallops for
2 or 3 minutes.

*See Kitchen Notes

Add in the lobster meat, the oregano, basil and black pepper. Remove from heat and drain off the juice, reserving it for the bêchamel sauce. Set the seafood in the refrigerator until needed.

To ASSEMBLE THE LASAGNA:

Cook the pasta according to package directions and immerse in ice water until you are ready to use it.

Mix together the ricotta cheese, the Parmesan cheese, the eggs and parsley.

In a 10-by-13 inch glass baking dish begin with a layer of marinara sauce and lay in a layer of cooked lasagna.

Spread one third of the ricotta mix onto the pasta and imbed one third of the seafood mix into it. Top with lasagna, marinara and repeat the sequence until you have 3 seafood layers, then finish with a generous amount of marinara.

Cover lightly with foil and bake at 350° F for 45 minutes. Remove foil, sprinkle with mozzarella and continue cooking for another 15 minutes.

Keep in mind that lasagna should have time to set up after cooking. Allow an extra 30 to 40 minutes if you can.

To MAKE THE BÊCHAMEL SAUCE:

In a medium saucepan, melt the butter over medium heat. Add in the flour and cook, stirring, for 4 minutes. Slowly pour in the fish stock, stirring with a wire whisk to eliminate lumps.

When the sauce is quite hot, stir in the tomato purée, along with the salt, pepper, nutmeg and basil.

Just before serving, add in the cream and heat it, taking care not to let the sauce boil as it will curdle.

To SERVE THE LASAGNA:

Cut the lasagna into portions, set on plates, and ladle the sauce over it. Garnish with fresh basil leaves.

Cod Steaks
with Sundried Tomato Butter

Serves 4

COD STEAKS ARE RARELY FOUND on fish counters today, but they may be custom cut at a good fish market. The flavor and moisture retained by serving this style are worth the trouble of avoiding bones.

4 8-ounce codfish steaks, 1-inch thick

Salt & pepper, to taste   *1 tablespoon olive oil*

FOR THE SUNDRIED TOMATO BUTTER:

3 tablespoons chopped (oil-packed) sundried tomatoes

¼ pound butter   *1 teaspoon chopped black olives*
½ teaspoon garlic paste   *1 tablespoon fresh chopped basil*
1 teaspoon anchovy paste

TO PREPARE THE SUNDRIED TOMATO BUTTER:

Allow the butter to soften at room temperature.

In a small bowl, mash all ingredients together until well blended.

Refrigerate the butter for an hour, then put it on a 12-inch square of plastic wrap. Fold the plastic over the butter and, with as little handling as possible, form it into a short roll about 1½ inches in diameter. Wrap it in the remaining plastic wrap and refrigerate until firm.

TO PREPARE THE COD STEAKS:

Brush the fish with olive oil, sprinkle with salt and pepper on both sides, then broil for 5 minutes per side.

Any remaining sundried tomato butter may be frozen for use at another time. It is very good on grilled meat or chicken, as well as on pasta or rice.

200

When the fish is done, put it onto plates and top with a slice of the sundried tomato butter.

Serve quickly before the butter melts.

Cuban Mahi-Mahi Dinner

Serves 6

WE HAVE ENJOYED MANY DINNERS in Cuban restaurants in Key West. Typically, the meal involves yellow rice, black beans, fried plantains, along with a garnish of lettuce, ripe tomato, and sliced onion. The secret to the Cuban flavoring used on fish, chicken, or pork is the Mojo Sauce. The recipe that follows can be used with any of the southern fish: grouper, snapper, bonito, or mahi-mahi. Cook it on the grill or in your oven, the aroma will certainly whet your appetite.

> *3 pounds mahi-mahi or other Caribbean fish*

FOR THE MOJO SAUCE:

> *½ cup finely diced onion*   *½ bay leaf*
> *1 tablespoon minced garlic*   *¼ teaspoon black pepper*
> *½ cup olive oil*   *1 teaspoon salt*
> *2 teaspoons vinegar*   *¼ cup lime juice*
> *¾ teaspoon oregano*   *¼ cup water*
> *¾ teaspoon ground cumin*   *¼ cup sherry*

TO PREPARE THE MOJO SAUCE:

In a small saucepan, simmer all the sauce ingredients for 10 minutes.

Cool the sauce, then process for only 30 seconds in the blender. There should be recognizable bits of onion left.

TO PREPARE THE MAHI-MAHI:

Preheat oven to 400° F.

Ladle 3 to 4 tablespoons of the sauce onto the bottom of a shallow baking pan, preferably glass. Lay the fish onto the sauce, then top with more sauce, using about half of the sauce for cooking the fish and saving the other half for the table.

Bake for 20 minutes, then check to see if it is done. Cooked fish will flake easily with a fork.

Baked Scrod
with Mushroom-Miso Sauce

Serves 4

MISO IS A JAPANESE PASTE that adds a rich flavor element to the mild taste of cod.

2 pounds scrod or other white fish fillet

FOR THE MUSHROOM-MISO SAUCE:
1 tablespoon olive oil
2 large shallots, diced
8 medium mushrooms, sliced
1 tablespoon flour
1 tablespoon miso, dissolved in 1 cup boiling water
2 tablespoons sherry
Fresh ground black pepper, to taste

Chopped scallions for garnish

TO PREPARE THE MUSHROOM-MISO SAUCE:
Sauté the shallots and mushrooms in olive oil until shallots are clear.
Sprinkle flour into the pan, allow it to heat, then add the miso broth. Cook, stirring frequently, for 5 minutes.
Stir in the sherry, then season with the pepper.
Lay the fish in a baking dish just big enough to contain the fish. Cover the fish with the sauce and bake in a preheated oven at 400° F for 20 minutes.

Seafood Mornay

Serves 8

HERE'S A SIMPLE SEAFOOD SAMPLER for people who would like to try a little of everything.

1½ pounds fillet of cod or haddock (skinned)*
½ pound scallops
½ pound uncooked shrimp, peeled & deveined*
½ pound cooked lobster meat

FOR THE MORNAY SAUCE:

¼ cup minced shallots	*1 cup fish stock*
2 tablespoons butter	*1 cup light cream*
3 tablespoons flour	*Pinch white pepper*
2 ounces grated Gruyere cheese	*Salt, to taste*

TO POACH THE SEAFOOD:

Put the fish and scallops into a skillet with a cup of water and a pinch of thyme. Bring to a boil, then reduce the heat to maintain a simmer for 8 minutes.

Add in the shrimp and continue cooking until the fish is cooked through, another 3 or 4 minutes.

Drain off the cooking liquid, reserving it to add to the sauce. Set the fish aside until needed.

TO PREPARE THE MORNAY SAUCE:

In a small saucepan, melt the butter and add in the shallots. Cook

*See Kitchen Notes

205

until shallots are clear, then add the flour. Cook for another minute, then add in the hot fish stock, stirring constantly to eliminate lumps.

Add the cream, cheese, and white pepper. Cook on low heat, stirring frequently until cheese is melted and sauce is piping hot. Remove from heat.

To bake the seafood:

Arrange the seafood in a heavy baking dish, cover with the sauce, and sprinkle with buttered bread crumbs.

Bake at 400° F until heated through and the topping is golden brown.

Kitchen Notes

DETERMINING FRESHNESS

Selecting seafood can be a bewildering experience for the uninitiated. If you buy from a reputable fish market, it is perfectly acceptable to ask your fish dealer's recommendation. Ask what the dealer would take home that night. On the other hand, if you have a certain type of fish in mind, you would like to be able to see for yourself that it is fresh.

In general, the fillets of the white fish (such as COD, HADDOCK, SOLE, OCEAN CATFISH, and CUSK) should have a pearly white appearance and firm-looking flesh. Others, such as POLLOCK and FLOUNDER have a slightly grayer appearance which should be translucent. If you can view the fish whole, look for bright red gills and clear eyes, as opposed to foggy, sunken ones. Avoid fillets that are yellowing, dry looking, or crusty on the outer edges.

The colors of fish fade as the meat gets older. In TUNA, look for a deep, rich maroon flesh. If it is beginning to brown, the TUNA may still be good enough to cook; however, it would not be considered sushi quality. SWORDFISH can vary from pearly light pink to a deeper orange pink. In either case, the bloodline should be bright red. If the fish looks chalky and dull, it is not fresh and may even have been frozen. Sometimes in supermarket displays you can actually see saw marks on SWORDFISH that has been frozen in a chunk and cut into steaks with a band saw.

The same basic principals apply to SALMON, BLUEFISH, MACKEREL, and

SHARK. The fish should look translucent and glisten with deep rich color. SHARK is the most perishable of all fish. Ask your fishmonger for assurances of quality. The key question should be: "Would *you* eat it?"

There is a wide range of quality in SCALLOPS on the market today. To the practiced eye, the difference is immediately obvious. Good, dry packed scallops will look firm and have some variation in the color of the individual meats. Fresh SEA SCALLOPS (as opposed to frozen) do have an odor which is off-putting. In the business, we call it "scallop gas". It is quite natural and has nothing to do with freshness. SCALLOPS that have been soaked to increase their weight will look flaccid, as though they are melting together, and the color will be a uniform white/gray. Look for milky liquid in the display dish, and you may suspect you have found SCALLOPS soaked in chemicals. Fresh CAPE SCALLOPS also give off a little milky liquid, but in our experience they're purchased so quickly that they never have a chance to get old on the fish counter.

As you begin to observe fish displays and compare supermarkets with seafood markets, picking out the freshest fish will become easier.

Above all, fresh fish should not have a strong odor. Remember, "If it smells like fish, it's bait!"

STORING SEAFOOD

Because they are highly perishable, fish and shellfish need to be kept as cold as possible. When you get the fish home, you should keep it in the coldest part of your refrigerator and remember to return the fish to the refrigerator between any stages of preparation.

If you need to keep the fish for more than a day or two, transfer it to a plastic, rather than paper wrap. LOBSTERS are the exception here. Though they should be kept in a paper bag, you should not store them longer than a day. And no matter what your well-intentioned friends might say, never attempt to keep LOBSTERS alive in water. They are saltwater creatures that need very cold, aerated water.

HANDLING SEAFOOD

With the well-regulated hazard controls now in place throughout the seafood industry, you can be assured that your seafood is safe whenever you buy from a reputable fishmonger. Once you get fish to your house, though, there are two simple principles to keep in mind: temperature control and cross-contamination.

Keep your seafood well chilled at every step of the operation from raw fish to cooked. Any fish will deteriorate faster at room temperature. Once the fish is warm it is not only diminishing in quality; it is allowing the rapid growth of naturally occurring bacteria. This is the source of food poisoning. It may help to remember that bacteria have about the same comfort zone as people: between 40° F and 110° F. When bacteria are in this comfort zone, they multiply. The simple rule: Keep hot foods hot and cold foods cold.

The second important concern in any kitchen preparation is cross-contamination. Every time you use a utensil or dish for uncooked fish you run the risk of transferring bacteria if you don't thoroughly wash that same utensil or dish before using it to handle some other food that will be eaten without further cooking.

This means that plate carrying the fish out to the grill must be washed before you place the cooked fish back upon it. A more exaggerated example of this would be if you pre- pared raw shrimp on a cutting board, then cut lettuce for a salad without ever having cleaned the same surface properly between the two kitchen tasks. Yet another example would be found in the refrigerator when juices from uncooked fish might drip into the lettuce.

Simple precautions will eliminate the possibility of these things happening in your kitchen. One is to clean your hands, knives, cutting boards, and dishes with hot, soapy water after handling or preparing fresh seafood. The other is to store fresh seafood in containers that will not allow the dripping of any juices.

Less obvious forms of cross-contamination are also just as easily prevented. Remember, any marinade used for fish must be discarded after its first and only use.

Please note that I have said that your seafood is safe when you buy it from a reputable fishmonger. If a neighbor brings CLAMS or OYSTERS he dug from a closed area, then you're on your own. The same goes for the weekend fisherman who leaves the BLUEFISH in the sun on the boat, keeps it overnight in his garage, then brings you a nice, fresh fish in the morning. Just say no.

Freezing Seafood

Whenever you must freeze seafood, follow a few simple procedures to prevent freezer burn. A serious hazard that affects the quality of frozen fish, freezer burn occurs when the seafood is exposed to the drying effects of the freezer atmosphere.

To keep the frigid air away from uncooked fish, we give it a protective coating of lightly-salted water. To make your own solution, dissolve ½ teaspoon of salt into 1 cup of water.

If you are freezing SCALLOPS, put them into a plastic container, cover them with the salted water, then jostle the container once or twice so the water will travel down into the air spaces.

Freezing uncooked fillets utilizes the same principal. Place the fillet flat inside a plastic bag. Keeping the bottom of the bag on the counter, pour in just enough salted water to surround the fish. Starting at the end with the fish in it, fold the bag over a few times, then lay it on a flat baking dish in such a way the water will not flow out.

If you need to freeze more than one piece of fish, divide them into serving sizes and freeze each in a separate bag. Set the bags on a baking sheet to freeze. Once frozen, the packets should be stored in a single layer so they don't freeze together.

When defrosting anything frozen in salted water, always discard the water and give the fish a quick rinse. It goes without saying that a person on a sodium-restricted diet would not choose this method of freezing.

Though cooked lobster meat does freeze well in the salt solution, cooked seafood generally fares better when tightly encased in plastic wrap. Leftovers that will be used in soups or stews can be stored in plastic containers and covered with a bit of fish stock or clam juice.

Defrosting Seafood

Obviously, it is preferable to use fresh fish exclusively; however, that is not always possible. To maintain the quality of any properly frozen seafood, care must be taken to defrost it correctly. The best method is to move the item from the freezer to the refrigerator 24 hours before needed. If you have the foresight to do this, simply place the frozen item in a pan to collect any water that may result from the thawing, and you are all set.

For the 98 per cent of us, who will not be planning the meal that far in advance, more drastic measures must be employed. In this case, the preferred method would be to place the fish into a sturdy plastic bag, then immerse it in cold water. For best results, use a lot of water and force the bag under the water by putting a weight of some sort on top.

Be aware of two important things. One is that most fish readily absorb fresh water and should never be soaked unless in a bag. The other is that warm or hot water must never be used, because it encourages the rapid proliferation of the bacteria naturally present in any fish or shellfish.

A possible exception to using a plastic bag would be when defrosting SQUID or SHRIMP in the shell. If you need only a few SQUID or SHRIMP from a large frozen block, set the block in a colander under cold running water until you are able to break away as many as you need.

While a microwave can be used to defrost fish, be careful not to actually cook some areas while leaving others frozen. The microwave can be used effectively if you set the timer for very short increments, then turn, rearrange, and break down the frozen mass as you go along.

If you have a pint of CHOPPED CLAMS, for example, set the timer for 45 seconds just to loosen the CLAMS from their original container. Then turn the semi-frozen lump into a low flat bowl and microwave it another 45 seconds. At this point, you may be able to cut the whole thing into four segments, microwave it again, and so on until the CLAMS are loose enough to use, yet not cooked. This method works well with frozen cooked LOBSTER or CRABMEAT, but not for uncooked SHRIMP.

PREPARING FISH FOR COOKING

It is always a good idea to inspect your finfish for bones before you cook it. This can be done by carefully running your finger along the length of the fillet, down the center of the non-skin side. Even if the skin is not on the fish, it is easy to tell which is the skin side by the silvery-gray tone left when the skin was removed. There may also be bones up near the nape of the flatfish (FLOUNDER and SOLE). Again, these can be located with a light touch of the fingers. The bones can usually be removed easily by hand, but in some cases you may need to use a small pair of pliers. Bones are rarely found in the larger fish, such as BASS and TUNA, but you would definitely need pliers to pull any out.

When preparing CRABMEAT or OYSTER dishes, watch for bits of shell, which can be picked-out manually.

Scallops should be checked for bits of shell or grit. These tiny inedible contaminants can be dealt with quite easily. For each pound of scallops, mix 2 teaspoons of salt with 4 cups of water in a medium-sized bowl. Add the scallops and move them around in the water so that the grit and shells fall to the bottom of the dish. Carefully lift the scallops and drain them in a colander. This same method can be used for cooked or raw, shucked clams, as well as cooked, shucked mussels.

It is said that fresh water is the enemy of dead fish. If you feel it necessary to rinse fish, mix a solution of 1 teaspoon salt to 2 cups cold water, dip the fish quickly, then pat it dry with paper towels.

SKINNING FINFISH

If a recipe calls for skinned fish, you can request it of the fish market, or you can skin it yourself without much difficulty.

Lay the fillet flat on a cutting board, close to the edge of the counter. Holding the tail end firmly with your left hand, begin at the tail end to cut into the flesh: first directing the blade toward the skin side, then laying it at an angle almost parallel to the cutting board. Hold the knife at this angle and simultaneously begin making sawing motions back and forth while pulling the skin piece off to the left. The knife should stay almost parallel to the cutting board, while the skin is being pulled along, separating it from the flesh of the fish. With practice, this skill will become easier.

In the case of larger fish, such as swordfish, tuna, and halibut, the skin can most easily be removed after the fish is cooked. Simply take a sharp knife and run it around the edge of the steak, separating the skin from the meat. The same applies to uncooked large fish, but the bond between skin and flesh is a bit stronger and takes more effort to remove.

COOKING FISH

In general, fish cooks very quickly. In the oven, on the grill, or in a sauté pan, the same rule of thumb applies: allow 10 minutes cooking for each inch of thickness. If you have added any stuffing to the basic fillet, you will need to adjust the time. Be aware, however, that it is far easier to overcook than undercook your fish. Even after the seafood has been removed from the direct source of heat, some cooking may continue. If you're new to the game, be over-cautious. You'll catch on to timing.

Checking for Doneness

There are a several ways to check your fish to be sure it is cooked through. The most reliable method is to actually look into it. Each fish will have a slightly different texture, but this method can be used reliably for everything from sole to scallops to swordfish. Insert a small sharp knife into the fish at the thickest point and check the flesh there. If it is done, the flesh will be opaque, and the meat will flake easily where it has been disturbed by the knife. If the fish is not done, the interior will be a translucent gray, and the flesh will feel firm and somewhat gummy.

A quick way to check the larger fish, (swordfish, shark, tuna, etc.) is to pierce it with a skewer or a small sharp knife. In the restaurant, we refer to it as a "scrodprod." This works especially well if you are cooking on the grill and the light is not strong enough for a visual check. If the fish is cooked, the skewer will go through the thickest part as though it were butter. If the fish is not quite done, the skewer will meet resistance, and you have to cook it a little longer. To get the feeling for doneness using this method, first check a thin section of the fish, then go to a thicker part. You should feel the difference right away.

Since there are always a variety of factors that influence cooking time, I am usually reluctant to prescribe exact cooking times. When people ask me how long to cook fish, I have to respond: "Until it's done!"

Making Fish Stock

Though commercial stocks and bouillon cubes are readily available in supermarkets, keep in mind that they might be saltier than this one. This stock can be made anytime and frozen in 1-pint containers.

Fish Stock

1 medium fish frame (from a 4lb or 5lb COD, HADDOCK, *or* POLLOCK)
Pinch of thyme

10 black peppercorns
1 onion, quartered
2 stalks of celery, cut in chunks
1 carrot, cut in chunks
4 sprigs of parsley
1 small bay leaf

Cut the fish frame in 2 or 3 pieces so that it will fit into a 10-quart pot.

Add the vegetables and herbs, then cover with cold water.

Bring the contents almost to a boil and reduce the heat slightly to simmer for about 40 minutes.

Strain the stock first through a colander, then through a strainer lined with cheesecloth.

Pour it into pint containers, allow it to cool, then place it on a flat surface in the freezer.

About Mussels

Mussels are indeed an under-appreciated local treasure! While their popularity is growing in the United States, they have been enjoyed by gourmets in other parts of the world for a long time. Their full hearty flavor and versatility make them a culinary delight for seafood lovers and cooks alike. Though mussels vary in size, they average 10 to 18 per pound; a serving would be about 1½ pounds (as weighed in the shell).

Mussels do require a little extra care in handling, however, and we must be diligent about inspecting and cleaning them. Mussels tend to gape or open even shortly after being taken from the water. If you pinch a mussel's two shells together, and they close up again (however slowly), the mussel is alive and fine to use. On the other hand, if the mussel doesn't respond, it is dead and must be discarded.

The mussels whose shells are held together tightly must also be scrutinized carefully, because some of them may be full of mud. To let a "mudder" get by your inspection is to destroy an entire dish. The damage is usually discovered at the last possible moment when it is too late to make corrections.

In the case of closed mussels, the dead ones can be detected by holding each mussel firmly in one hand and attempting to slide one shell over the other, using a slight, twisting motion. If it is a mudder, the top shell will slide right off, and a culinary disaster will be avoided.

Cleaning Mussels

Once the preliminary inspection has been completed, and the dead mussels are safely in the garbage bin, you will need to clean the shells of seaweed and the little bits of grit you will likely find. I usually set up a two-part operation in the sink: one pan of water for the wash, and a colander to drain them after. Set the mussels beside your wash water, then dip them one by one into the pan while scrubbing each lightly with a small, stiff brush. This should be enough to clean them, but once in a while you may come across a barnacle that should be removed with a small, sharp knife. (A clam knife is ideal if you have one.) Drain the cleaned mussels in the colander.

Whenever a recipe calls for mussels to be cooked in the shell, you need to de-beard them beforehand. Simply use your fingers to pull-off the small clump of tough fibers that the mussel uses to attach itself to rocks. If you will be using only the mussel meats out of the shell, it is easier to remove the beards after they have been steamed.

STEAMING MUSSELS

To steam the mussels, it's better if you choose a pan that is flat and shallow rather than tall and deep, put about 1 inch of water in the bottom. Cover it, then heat until boiling.

Add the mussels and cook for 5 to 10 minutes, or until all the shells are open.

Drain the broth (this can be used in your recipe or frozen for use later as a fish stock) and refrigerate the mussels in a shallow pan.

When they are cool enough to handle, they can be removed from the shell. First, pinch the beard between your fingers and pull it away, while you squeeze the 2 shells gently together to hold the meat in. Next, pull the mussel from the shell and place the meat into a container. Be sure to keep these mussel meats cold until you are ready to use them.

OPENING OYSTERS

Probably the safest method of opening oysters is to use a simple "church key" can opener. First, locate the hinge at the narrow end of the oyster shell, where the top and bottom halves are joined together. Place the oyster on a stable surface, cover it with a dish towel, then use the pointed end of the church key to pry open the rear hinge. Once you get the oyster to pop open, simply reach in with a paring knife and cut the single muscle that attaches the oyster to both halves of the shell. And please, don't cut the oyster meat.

PEELING & DEVEINING SHRIMP

Shrimp can be peeled and cleaned either by hand, or by using a plastic shrimp peeler. Holding the tail segment firmly with your left hand, use your right hand to peel apart the shell where the back section joins the leg sections. Loosen this back shell by working your way from the tail toward the head end. After all the back shell segments have been removed, pull off the legs. In some cases you may wish to leave the last section and the tail on the shrimp. If not, they can be taken off next.

To remove the vein, make a shallow cut along the outer, top side of the peeled shrimp and pull out the sand vein. In some cases the vein may be very hard to see. This is not a problem; it's been flushed clean, and you need not worry about it further.

COOKING LOBSTERS

Begin with about 2 inches of water in the pot and bring to a boil.

Add lobsters.

When the water returns to a boil, begin the timed cooking:

LOBSTER SIZE	FROM SECOND BOIL
1 to 1¼ lbs	15 minutes
1½ lbs	18 minutes
1¾ to 2¼	20 minutes
2¼ to 3¼	25 minutes
3½ to 4¾	30 minutes
5 lbs	35 minutes
8 lbs	40 minutes

For larger lobsters, add 5 min/lb to the cooking time. Remember, the larger lobsters are tough only if they are undercooked.

To tell if a lobster is done, hold it by the back, pull the tail away from the body. If it snaps back it's undercooked. If it goes back slowly, it's cooked.

CLEANING LOBSTERS

Begin by removing the tail from the body, which is done simply by bending the top of the tail backward from the bottom of the body.

The meat of the tail can be removed in a couple of ways. One is to cut through the bottom of the tail with a pair of kitchen shears, then remove the meat. The other is to break off the tail fan, then force a fork or your finger into the tail and push the meat out the other end.

Remove the claws by twisting their "knuckles" (or arms) free from the body. The meat from the claws and knuckles can best be reached by breaking the shell with a lobster cracker, then removing the meat with a pick.

Only the most patient folks will then work their way through the body itself to the precious, tiny pieces of meat deep between the gills, as well as the tomalley and roe. The best way to benefit from the 8 legs is simply to break each at their joints and suck out the meat.

Opening Clams (Quahogs)

This heading is sort of deceiving, because any Cape & Islands local will tell you that SOFTSHELL CLAMS are only opened by steaming; hence, the name STEAMERS. But HARDSHELL CLAMS, QUAHOGS, are shucked raw for eating and for stuffing. Of course, they can also be steamed like MUSSELS.

As for shucking a hardshell clam, this is a talent that is just a bit easier than shucking the rough and reluctant OYSTER. At least the oyster, though, can be opened with a "church key."

There are 4 key elements to this QUAHOG procedure: a strong clam knife, which is available in most culinary or hardware stores; a clean bowl in which to catch the liquor; a glove that can provide a good grip of the shell, as well as protect your hand from the knife; and a tray of crushed ice. If you place the QUA-HOGS undisturbed on the ice for a few minutes, they will relax a bit and provide just enough more of an opening between their shells to make it easier to insert your knife.

Keeping in mind that you don't want to startle the CLAM into closing its shell any tighter, take the QUAHOG in the palm of your gloved hand so that the hinge of its 2 shells fits snugly against the base of your thumb.

Insert the sharp edge of your knife into the groove between the 2 shells, then wrap the fingers of your gloved hand around the dull edge of the blade.

Carefully apply firm pressure with your gloved fingers to force the sharp edge of your knife through the groove and into the QUAHOG's shells.

Once the knife is inside, run the blade deeper around the perimeter to cut the muscles that hold the shells closed. If the CLAM should try to clamp down on your blade, a simple twist of the knife is enough to open up the QUAHOG wide enough to see the muscles inside.

What happens next depends upon your recipe.

Cleaning Squid

Before cleaning squid for a recipe, keep in mind that it takes 1½ lbs of uncleaned squid to yield 1 lb of clean squid.

Begin by separating the tentacles and head from the body. Grabbing the squid gently behind the eyes, pull the tentacles and head out of the body. Be aware of the fact that squid does have a sack of black ink within that you will encounter either at this point, or when you clean the body. Disregarding the innards for the moment, push the tentacles apart so that you can find the mouth at their base. You should be able to feel the beak with your fingertip and to remove it with a squeeze between your two thumbnails. Once it pops-up, simply pull the beak out.

Next, make a clean slice between the eyes and the tentacles, then discard the head and the connected innards. Generally, the tentacles are kept as one piece.

Cleaning the body is even easier. Use your fingers to feel inside the body cavity for the clear piece of long, narrow, flat cartilage that looks very much like a piece of plastic. Take it out and throw it away. Finally, remove the thin skin of the squid by first scratching the body with your thumbnail, then peeling away the skin. When you're done, rinse thoroughly. Some recipes will call for the body to be sliced into rings; others, to be kept whole.

Making Drawn Butter

Melt the butter, then let it harden in the refrigerator so that the milk solids will settle to the bottom. Poke a hole in the solidified butter and drain off the liquid.

Invert the container and lightly scrape the white solids from the bottom of the mass. You are left with clarified butter which can be used for cooking or dipping lobsters, steamers, artichokes, etc.

Glossary of the Fishes

THIS LIST OF FISH and shellfish is by no means complete. Of the 20,000 known species of bony fish, we have selected those which are commonly caught off the Northeast coast of the United States, some Southern species, and assorted others which are included in the recipes in this book.

Alewife: *See* RIVER HERRING.

American Herring: Unlike RIVER HERRING that spawn upstream, this fish spends its entire life at sea. Young are called SARDINES.

American Lobster: The superstar of New England seafood that is commonly — but not always accurately – called "Maine lobster", it is found in rocky bottoms from Rhode Island to Canada. Unlike the SPINY LOBSTER of warmer waters, this has two claws: a heavy crusher claw and a thinner ripper claw, used to catch and tear food. Hard-shelled until annual molting when it sheds its shell and grows larger, usually in the summer. Takes 7 years to grow to 1 pound size ("chicken lobsters" or "chix"), then a year per pound after. Firm white flesh with rich sweet flavor. A "cull" is a lobster with one claw, and a "bullet" has lost both claws.

Arctic Char: A freshwater fish, related to the TROUT; market weight about 1 pound. Fine grained, orange flesh, delicate flavor.

Atlantic Mackerel: A beautiful, sleek multi-colored fish, usually 1 to 2 pounds. Strong flavor, dark oily flesh, delicious when very fresh.

Trap mackerel, caught near shore in spring are considered the best.

Bass: A large family of fish including fresh and salt water varieties. See Striped Bass, Chilean Sea Bass, Hybrid Bass.

Bay Scallop: *See* Cape Scallop.

Blackback: A smaller-sized Winter Flounder.

Blue Crab: Hard shell, except in spring and summer when they shed and are sold as "Softshell Crab". Source of lump meat, jumbo lump, and back fin. Range from Florida to Cape cod. Prime commercial harvest is from the Chesapeake Bay and the Southern states.

Bluefin Tuna: The largest and most prized of the species. Once sold as "horse mackerel" for 5¢ a pound, bluefin now commands prices as high as $30,000 per fish.

Bluefish: Range from northern Florida to the southern Gulf of Maine. Bluefish migrate to the Cape Cod area in late spring. Dark flesh with high oil content. Average size is 3 to 6 pounds. One of the best fighting game fish in our waters.

Blue Tip Shark: Not very good eating. Wreaks havoc with long-line fishermen.

Boston Bluefish: A marketing term given to Pollock, no longer in common usage. No relation to true Bluefish.

Calamari: *See* Squid.

Cape Scallop: Harvested in fall and winter from shallow rivers and bays throughout the Cape & Islands. It is prized for its sweet tender meat.

Catfish: *See* Ocean Catfish.

Cero Mackerel: Southern cousin of the Atlantic Mackerel, found occasionally in northern waters in the summer.

Chilean Sea Bass: A sweet mild, flesh, large flake. Most similar to Halibut in taste and texture.

Cobia: A large game fish from Southern waters. Great fighter, looks like a Shark in the water. Closest to Grouper in taste.

Cod: A groundfish found in the North Atlantic, white flesh with a mild flavor.
    Scrod: Cod up to 4 pounds.
    Market: Cod 4 to 10 pounds.

LARGE: COD 12 to 25 pounds.

STEAKER: Very large cod without the head.

WHALE: COD 25 pounds and up.

Clams: Live buried in the sand or mud and feed by siphoning food through a tube or "foot". There are dozens of varieties around the world, but for the clams of culinary value on the Cape & Islands, *See* QUAHOG, RAZOR CLAM, SEA CLAM, STEAMER CLAM, SURF CLAM.

Crabs: *See* BLUE CRAB, MAINE CRABMEAT, ROCK CRAB, STONE CRAB.

Conch: (pronounced Konk) The classic shell from which to hear the ocean roar, this seafood is no longer harvested in Florida. Source is now Bahamas and Philippines. Meat is chewy, usually ground or pounded before cooking.

Cusk: Long slender fish, bycatch and cousin of the COD. Sweet, firm meat with excellent mild flavor.

Dab: (Gray Sole) Plentiful in Gulf of Maine and Cape & Islands. Averages 1 to 3 pounds. Mild flavor.

Dogfish: *See* SPINY DOGFISH *and* SHARK.

Dolphin Fish: *See* MAHI-MAHI.

Dorado: *See* MAHI-MAHI.

Dover Sole: Large member of the FLOUNDER family. Popular in Europe, imported from England and Holland. Often cooked whole. Delicate white flesh.

Eel: Looks like a snake, but this is a true fish with scales, fins, and gills. Particularly relished by Europeans. Caught by trap in local rivers in summer and fall. Excellent smoked.

Flounder: A family of flatfish found in both the Atlantic and Pacific. Local species are caught near Cape Cod shores or on Georges Bank. FLOUNDER have a confusing array of names, most SOLE is actually FLOUNDER. See BLACKBACKS, DAB, SUMMER FLOUNDER, FLUKE, GRAY SOLE, HALIBUT, SAND DAB, WINDOWPANE, YELLOWTAIL.

Gray Sole: Fillets 4 to 6 ounces. One of the most popular fish because of its subtle, sweet flavor. When fresh, it smells like cucumber. *See* FLOUNDER.

Grouper: The COD of the south. A family of saltwater fish found in temperate waters ranging in size from 3 to 600 pounds. Average weight 5 to 10 pounds. Strong flavor, denser meat than most northern species. Varieties include RED GROUPER, BLACK GROUPER, and SCAMP GROUPER.

Haddock: Similar to COD, delicate white meat. Once the staple fish of New England diet, over fished in the 1980's, rebounded in recent years.

Halibut: The Cadillac of white fish; largest member of the FLOUNDER family found in the Atlantic and Pacific. The largest of the species (100 to 150 lbs), once a common catch at the turn of the 20th century, are rarely seen today. Average size 40 to 80 pounds. Meat is firm and mild with a large flake.

Hake: Close relative to the COD but smaller, not as important commercially. Meat is mild, soft, off-white color.

Herring: See ALWIFE, AMERICAN HERRING, RIVER HERRING.

Hybrid Bass: A new species, looks like a short, stocky STRIPED BASS. Farmed and sold commercially year round.

King Mackerel: (Kingfish) Large

tropical variety, teeth like a barracuda. Strong flavor, excellent grilled or smoked.

Lane Snapper: Very tasty, small fish, sometimes sold as "Red Snapper".

Lemon Shark: Smaller, southern species; good eating.

Lemon Sole: Large WINTER FLOUNDER, not as common as GRAY SOLE.

Lobster: See AMERICAN LOBSTER, MAINE LOBSTER, SPINY LOBSTER.

Lotte: French name for MONKFISH. Commonly used in bouillabaisse.

Mackerel: See ATLANTIC MACKEREL, CERO MACKEREL, KING MACKEREL, TINKER MACKEREL, SPANISH MACKEREL.

Mahi-Mahi: (Dolphin Fish or Dorado) Rainbow colors when taken from the ocean. Very agreeable flavor, mild and moist when fresh. Plentiful in Florida, Central and South America and Hawaii.

Maine Crabmeat: Sold out of the shell from crabs known locally as "Quick Crabs", "Sand Crabs", or dubbed by Maine tourists as "Picky

Toe Crabs". Sweet tender meat.

Mako Shark: Most prized for quality eating. Similar to SWORDFISH, but milder and more moist. A large and aggressive variety.

Monkfish: (Goose Fish or Lotte) A member of the ANGLER FISH family, it has a huge head, wide mouth, and conical body whose tail which is the edible portion of this ugly fish. Cooked properly it is excellent. Flavor and texture of meat has earned the nick name "Poor Man's Lobster".

Mullet: Blueish-gray with large scales average 2 to 3 pounds. Travel in schools, common in Florida.

Mussels: Until recently, an overlooked treasure of our cold waters. Black/blue shell with tender orange meats, flavor a little stronger than CLAM. Attach themselves to rocks or shells with strong fibres called a "beard" which should be removed before eating. MUSSELS are being farmed with great success in Maine where they are grown on ropes suspended in the water.

Mutton Snapper: One of the larger snappers, olive green with brick red gills.

Ocean Catfish: (Wolfish) Totally different from fresh water CATFISH. It has a long body and fierce appearance with jagged teeth. Average size 6 to 10 pounds. White meat, similar to COD, but firmer. Great in soups and stews.

Ocean Perch: Red fish, not to be confused with RED SNAPPER. Color is pinkish red with large black eyes, Average 2 pounds. Meat is firm with delicate flavor.

Oysters: The champagne of shellfish, their coarse shells yield nutty, briny, tender meats. Every town on Cape & Islands has an oyster named for it. Each varies in saltiness, firmness, and shell shape. "Wellfleets" and "Chathams" are tops in *our* book. Sold in the shell or shucked. Eaten raw or cooked. Other varieties include MELPEQUES, BELAN, and BLUEPOINT.

Pollock: Related to the COD with darker, softer flesh. Size from 3 to 10 pounds. Atlantic species abundant in the Gulf of Maine. Sometimes marketed as BOSTON BLUEFISH although unrelated to the BLUEFISH. ALASKAN POLLOCK is used in the making of sushimi or "mock crabmeat".

Porbeagle Shark: Similar to Mako, but smaller and not as firm.

Quahog: (pronounced KOE-hog) A family of hardshell clams cooked in chowders, stuffed or eaten raw.

 Littlenecks: (1 inch deep) can be eaten raw or steamed. Top necks are the largest of these.

 Cherrystones: (2½ to 3 in. dia) can be eaten raw or cooked.

 Chowder Clams: (3+ in. dia) chopped for chowders or stuffed.

Razor Clam: A long, thin clam up to 6 inches long. Sweet meat, chewy texture. A minor local market for these bivalves, so most are shipped off-Cape.

Red Snapper: Made famous by Chef Paul Prudhomme, who features these fish pan blackened. *See* Snapper.

River Herring: (Alewife) is a small fish, runs from ocean to freshwater origins to spawn in spring. Roe is a local delicacy. Flesh is oily and bony. It is usually smoked, pickled or brined.

Rock Crab: (Jonah Crab) A bycatch in Cape & Islands lobster pots, but of no great culinary value.

Roe: *See* Shad Roe.

Sand Dab: *See* Windowpane.

Sardine: *See* American Herring.

Salmon: Found on the Atlantic and Pacific coasts, a firm flesh, pink to red in color. Average 10 to 12 pounds although the cohos are considerably smaller. Spend 2 to 3 years at sea before returning to fresh water to spawn. Very successfully farm raised in cold waters of northern Atlantic. Varieties include: Atlantic, Chinook, Coho.

Scallop: A family of bi-valves, found around the world. Unlike others, such as the Clam, the Scallop travels by snapping its shells closed and propelling itself backwards. Generally, only the adductor muscle is removed from the shell and eaten. Caught by dredging along the ocean bottom. Local varieties include the Cape (Bay) Scallop and the Sea Scallop. Other varieties: Calico Bay, Digby Bay, China Bay, Icelandic.

Schrod: *See* Cod. An old fashioned menu term, used to describe a thick cut of cod baked with crumbs. "Boston hotel-style schrod".

Scrod: Small fish from the COD, HADDOCK, or POLLOCK family. Term has become interchangeable with COD.

Scup: (Porgy) A small, compact bony fish taken in summer. Very popular with Mediterraneans. Often grilled whole. Sweet meat.

Sea Clam: (Surf Clam) Growing up to 8 inches long, they are harvested by dredge in Cape Cod Bay and deeper water offshore. The sweet, nutty meat is used in chowders and clam pies or cut in strips for frying.

Sea Scallop: Fished year round, offshore by large boats in deeper waters, this variety has a large flat pink shell and relatively large meats (5 to 40/lb).

Shad: Like the HERRING, SHAD lives in the ocean, returns to fresh water to spawn. Caught in rivers from Chesapeake Bay to New England. Flesh is oily and bony, usually discarded in favor or the ROE.

Shad Roe: Egg sacs from SHAD. Very popular delicacy.

Shark: Only in the last decade or so have North Americans eaten SHARK. It had always been the other way around. Varieties include: BLUE TIP SHARK, LEMON SHARK, MAKO SHARK, PORBEAGLE SHARK, SPINY DOGFISH, THRESHER SHARK.

Shrimp: There are dozens of types and grades on the market today, and 99% grow in tropical waters, where many are cultivated. SHRIMP is not a big commercial fishery in North America with a few delicious exceptions. Our favorites include the tiny MAINE SHRIMP, harvested in winter in the Gulf of Maine. KEY WEST PINK SHRIMP, brought in year round from the Gulf of Mexico, are a top quality shrimp; tender, plump and sweet. North Carolina also boasts a shrimp fishery. During the summer they are available fresh and can't be beat.

Silver Hake: *See* WHITING.

Smelt: Lives in fresh or salt water. A small (4- to 7-inch), bony fish. High fat content; sweet mild flavor.

Snapper: Second only to GROUPER as the most common catch in Florida. Average size is 1 to 4 pounds. Varieties abundant in southern waters. *See* LANE SNAPPER, MUTTON SNAPPER, RED SNAPPER, YELLOWTAIL SNAPPER.

Sole: Flatfish, bottom dwelling, member of the FLOUNDER family. Delicate white flesh. *See* DOVER SOLE, GRAY SOLE, LEMON SOLE.

Spiny Dogfish: Small "Sand Shark" usually exported to Europe and Asia.

Spanish Mackerel: A speedy, warm water MACKEREL, mild flavor.

Spiny Lobsters: Clawless species found in warm southern waters. Bland flavor. Frozen lobster tails are frequently imported from South Africa or New Zealand.

Squid: Seen on menus as CALAMARI. A member of the MOLLUSK family, fished around the world. Possibly the only seafood which benefits from freezing, which tenderizes it. Tubes and tentacles are eaten.

Summer Flounder: (Fluke) Slightly dry but most preferred by residents of the mid-Atlantic states. An excellent game fish.

Steamer Clam: Softshell clams eaten steamed *au natural* or else shucked and fried.

Stone Crab: Found from Florida to the Carolinas. Only one claw is har-vested at a time, making these a con-stantly renewable resource. Sweet fla-vor, similar to lobster.

Striped Bass: A prized game fish, ranges from the Carolinas to Maine, migrating seasonally. The fish weigh up to 40 or 50 pounds. The meat is firm, slightly fatty, with a rich sweet taste.

Swordfish: A large migratory fish, averages 100 to 200 pounds, but may grow up to 400 pounds. Ranges from South America to Canada. Firm sweet flesh, pink or tan with maroon center section. Usually sold in steaks or rounds. Every meat-eater's favorite fish.

Tautog: A member of the CUNNER family, heavy, stout-bodied fish av-erages 3 to 5 pounds. A fish prized by Mediterranean cultures, usually shipped from Cape to New York City. Makes great fish chowder.

Thresher Shark: A Pacific variety, considered good eating.

Tilefish: A brightly-colored fish found from Gulf of Mexico to Nova Scotia, although it prefers the warmer waters. Meat is firm, white and flaky.

Tilapia: A tropical fresh water fish now farm raised around the world. Bland, soft, white meat.

Tinker Mackerel: Baby MACKEREL, under 1 pound, cooked whole.

Triple tail: Caught in Florida and south. A substitute for GROUPER.

Trout: Fresh water fish, small with fine grained flesh and sweet flavor. Often farm raised, to stock fishing ponds or to be sold commercially.

Tuna: A member of the MACKEREL family, found in all the world's oceans. The flesh is deep red with a texture like beef. Fish caught in colder waters or late in the fall have a higher fat content, therefore a better taste. Best cooked lightly, or served as sushi. Varieties include: ALBACORE, BIG-EYE, BLUEFIN TUNA, MEDITERRANEAN, SKIPJACK.

Turbot: (Final *t* is silent) Flatfish, weighing up to 30 pounds, found off the coast of Europe and in the Mediterranean. Firm white flesh, delicate flavor.

Wahoo: (Ono) Relative of the MACKEREL, a great sportfish off Hawaii. Large fish, average market weight 20 to 40 pounds, usually sold steaked. Good substitute for SWORDFISH, great on the grill.

Whiting: (Silver Hake) A small fish, one half to three pounds, sold whole. Delicate, soft white meat.

Windowpane: (Sand Dab) A very thin fish; it is said if you hold it up you can see light through it. Average 8 oz to 1½ pounds.

Winter Flounder: Smaller fish are called BLACKBACKS. As fish grow, white underside turns yellow. Because of the coloring, WINTER SOLE over 3 pounds have been given the marketing name LEMON SOLE. They are the thickest, meatiest of the East Coast FLOUNDER. Smaller fish are caught from bridges and smallboats.

Wolfish: *See* OCEAN CATFISH.

Yellowtail Flounder: Landed on Cape Cod year round. Thin fillets have fine flake and delicate flavor. Average size 1½ pounds.

Yellowtail Snapper: Colorful with a bright yellow streak running to the tail. Popular eating fish. Largest, about 3 pounds are called "Flags".

Acknowledgments

THE TRUE HEART AND SOUL of this book can be found in the people who have worked at Swan River Fish Market & Restaurant over the years that we have been here. A seasonal business is a strange animal, and there is no business course available to prepare for such madness. Each year a crew of returnees comes together with a group of new faces to carry on the spirit of years past. Morale always builds, and everyone pulls together to deliver a great product under a great deal of stress.

No one person has set the tone and established the character of Swan River Fish Market over the past 30 years more than Jim Stone. Unfortunately, Jim passed away a few years ago. He was loved by customers and co-workers alike, because he truly cared about people. Kerry Cassin also helped set the standards of quality which we adhere to every day.

Over the years, the torch has been passed to new people as veteran employees guide them along. A special tip of the hat goes to Debbie Demetriou, Sue Warner, Glen Woodworth, Chuck (of-the-truck) Lawrence, and countless other long-term employees at Swan River.

We now have a new crew to thank, the folks operating our new baby, Swan River Seafoods in Naples, Florida. The tremendous success of our southern operation has pleased and surprised us. We are most indebted to Doug Woodworth, who helped make it happen from the start, along with Joe McLaughlin, Mark Davis, Christina, Pam, Destiny, Pablo, and many others.

Reina Diaz, our friend and backbone of the Naples business, deserves special commendation, along with many other hardworking employees from points south of Florida.

There have been literally hundreds of others who have toiled with us to put themselves through college or to get started with their lives. We enjoy nothing more than watching these young people come into Swanee at the age of 14 or 15, work and grow over their years here, then return as grown-ups with families of their own. We like to believe that we have helped somehow in our own way to help them in that sometimes difficult growth from teenagers to adults.

We would like to thank Charlotte Ventola for her help over the years in our own transition from employees to employers.

And we must thank our two fabulous sons, Eric and Brendan. They have had to deal with a lot of competition for their time during the making of this book, as well as the running of Swan River. They are the pride and joy of our lives.

Many others have helped us test the recipes and reread these fishtales. They are too numerous to mention, but we thank you all very much.

Finally, we would like to thank Fred Sargent and his late wife, Brenda. Fred's father, Capt. Don Sargent, founded Swan River Fish Market nearly fifty years ago, and Fred worked many years to establish Swan River as the great place that it is. We are forever in his debt for believing in us and allowing us the opportunity to continue what he and his father had started.

Thank you, one and all.

Index